The *Parents*™ Magazine Baby and Child-Care Series combines the most up-to-date medical findings, the advice of doctors and child psychologists, and the actual day-to-day experiences of parents like you. Covering a wide variety of subjects, these books answer all your questions, step-by-important-step, and provide the confidence of knowing you're doing the best for your child—with help from *Parents*™ Magazine.

"This is a terrific book! What I like best is the up-beat tone and the clarity of ideas. It's a really sane book—no gimmicks, just wonderfully readable and clearly based on what children are like. Ms. Cole really understands parents and knows how to talk to them. There will be a whole generation of children who will grow up and thank Joanna Cole."

> Nancy Balaban
> Director
> Program in Infant and Parent Development
> Bank Street College of Education

# Parents™

## Book of
# Toilet Teaching

## Joanna Cole

### Foreword by Dr. Fitzhugh Dodson

BALLANTINE BOOKS • NEW YORK

Copyright © 1983 by Parents Magazine Enterprises, a Division of Gruner + Jahr, U.S.A., Inc.

All rights reserved under International and Pan-American Copyright Conventions. Published in the United States by Ballantine Books, a division of Random House, Inc., New York, and simultaneously in Canada by Random House of Canada Limited, Toronto.

Grateful acknowledgment is made to the following for permission to reprint previously published material:
Alfred A. Knopf, Inc.: Excerpt from YOUR BABY AND CHILD: From Birth to Age Five by Penelope Leach. Copyright © 1977, 1978 by Dorling Kindersley, Ltd., London. Copyright © 1977, 1978 by Penelope Leach. Reprinted by permission of Alfred A. Knopf, Inc.

Delacorte Press/Seymour Lawrence: Excerpts from DOCTOR AND CHILD by T. Berry Brazelton. Copyright © 1976 by T. Berry Brazelton. Used by permission of Delacourt Press/Seymour Lawrence.

Pocket Books: Excerpt from BABY AND CHILD CARE by Dr. Benjamin Spock. Copyright © 1945, 1946, 1957, 1968 and 1976 by Benjamin Spock, M.D. Reprinted by permission of Pocket Books, a division of Simon and Schuster, a division of Gulf and Western Corporation.

Van Nostrand Reinhold Company, Inc.: From CHILDHOOD ENCOPRESIS AND ENURESIS by Charles E. Schaefer, Ph.D. Copyright © 1979 by Van Nostrand Reinhold Company, Inc. Reprinted by permission of Van Nostrand Reinhold Company.

Library of Congress Catalog Card Number: 82-91150

ISBN 0-345-34332-8

Manufactured in the United States of America

First Edition: July 1983
Eighteenth Printing: June 1993

# Contents

# Acknowledgments

The author would like to thank Janice P. Miller, Dr. Charles E. Schaefer, Dr. Leon Schein, Peggy Sradnick, and Dr. Patricia Stone for their expert help and advice in preparing this book. I am especially grateful to Dr. Schaefer for reviewing the manuscript for chapters 6 and 7.

Special thanks go to the parents who granted lengthy interviews about their children's toilet learning, and without whom this book would not be what it is.

I am grateful also to Jean Detière for transcribing the interview tapes with so much care and attention, and for her friendly interest in the project.

And finally thanks to Evelyn Podsiadlo for her sound editorial advice and support.

# A Word About This Book and How to Use It

"The book said kids will start staying dry for two hours at a time," said the mother of a toddler. "Mollie seems old enough, but her diaper is always wet."

"The book said you should wait until a child *wants* to use the potty," complained the father of two young boys. "Our first son was eager at twenty months, but Jason, our second, has no interest at all at thirty-five months."

"The book said..." I heard this phrase again and again in talking with parents about toilet teaching, and I realized that they felt the books had let them down. In general, child-care books devote a chapter or a section of a chapter, or sometimes just a few paragraphs, to toilet teaching. Each book says something valid and useful, but no book says quite enough. And to fill in the gaps, parents go to other parents for advice and information.

Indeed, the parents with whom I spoke often finished the stories that began with "The book said . . ." with remarks like ". . . so I asked my sister who has two kids in school," or ". . . I told another father who said they'd had the same trouble with their child," or ". . . I asked my mother and she said not to worry."

Once I had confirmed my suspicion that parents of toddlers first read the book for general principles and then consult others about details, I began to wonder if another kind of book was needed. One that would summarize the contribution of the experts—for there is now a significant body of research on toddlers and their development—and also report the experiences of parents like you and me. Therefore, in *Parents*™ *Book of Toilet Teaching*, you will find the wisdom of child psychologists and physicians supplemented by quotes from the many generous parents who were willing to share with me the emotions they went through and the knowledge they gained while helping their toddlers learn to use the toilet.

Possibly the advice given most frequently to parents about toilet teaching is to relax. I have always found this kind of advice annoying at worst, and useless at best. If I am about to fly a plane for the first time, I will probably feel nervous, and it won't help to be told to relax. What *will* help is some specific knowledge of how to work the plane and an idea of what to expect in the air. I'd also like an experienced guide to let me know when I'm making a mistake and when I'm on the right track. *Then* I will feel reassured and will be able to relax a bit.

It has been my aim to write this book so it will perform these functions for parents as they begin toilet teaching. I suggest reading the book through in order, especially chapters 2 through 6, which form a unit describing the process of toilet teaching from beginning to end. (*Please* do *not* follow the guide in chapter 4 for no more daytime diaper before reading chapter 2 on readiness and carrying out the steps in chapter 3 for preparing your child for toilet learning.) Before your child has completely mastered toileting, unexpected setbacks may arise, and you may need to refer again to chapter 7, "Common Difficulties During Toilet Learning," or chapter 5, "The Learning Period." You will find a small amount of repetition from chapter to chapter to reinforce essential information and to ensure that nothing important will be missing when you return to certain sections for specific problems.

During the months when I was researching, interviewing, and writing this book, I harbored the secret ambition that it would answer every question a parent could ever have about toilet teaching. No sooner was the manuscript completed, however, than this fantasy was exposed for the foolishness it was. For I kept hearing new stories of toilet-teaching problems and unique ways that parents and children had developed to handle them. At first, I would rush to the typewriter to try to squeeze in another paragraph before the deadline, and I suspect that this will always be my instinct when I hear something that makes me think, "That should be in chapter 4!" But by now I have accepted what anyone could have told me all along, that no book can tell you everything, nor should any book really try. Not only will you be confronted with specific details in real life that will not be covered in this book, you will also probably find that you disagree with some of its ideas. If you do, you should follow your own lights.

In general, however, I think you will find that the philosophy presented here is one of common sense and a balance between parents' rights and children's needs. I believe that the best approach to toilet teaching and most other child-rearing issues is to accept and understand a child where she is and to guide her through encouragement to where she is going. I hope the general principles given here will help you do that for your child.

I believe too that parents deserve and need understanding and encouragement, and I hope you will find some of both for yourself in this book as well.

# Foreword

### By Dr. Fitzhugh Dodson

I like to keep up with what my colleagues in child raising are saying. So several years ago I took, incognito, an evening course in parenting at UCLA, given by a Los Angeles psychiatrist. By the type of questions and comments from the audience I would guess that at least two-thirds of them were college-educated.

When we came to the section dealing with toilet teaching, I was dumbfounded by some of the questions. I remember one particularly vividly. A well-dressed woman raised her hand and asked, "When you're toilet training your child, is it all right to spank him if he keeps having accidents?" Other women chimed in, "Yes, yes, is it all right to spank?" The instructor explained why this was not a good idea, but I was really jolted by the questions. Surely these mothers wouldn't hire a piano teacher who spanked their child's hand when she made a mistake. But in all seriousness they wondered if it was all right to take a teaching process such as toilet learning and punish mistakes by spanking!

And yet as I thought more about it, it wasn't so surprising that parents know little about toilet teaching. And the reason they know so little is the same reason they know so little about overhauling the transmission in their cars. Nobody has taught them how to do it. Do they learn how to toilet teach from their own parents? No. And if they did it would be a classic case of the blind leading the blind. Do the schools teach them? No. But surely they can learn from books on child raising, can't they?

I have an extensive library of books on child raising. I just spent an afternoon going over each book in my collection, looking up the sections on toilet learning. I was absolutely astounded to find that many of the books had absolutely nothing on the subject. Nothing! Others contained gross errors. (One book recommended that you bowel train your youngster between nine and fourteen months, and the writer of the book was a psychoanalyst, if you can believe that!)

Then several books advanced the rather incredible notion that children can toilet train themselves. They say that once a child is two, she can train herself in a relatively short time. These authors claim they know lots of kids who've done this. I may be very naïve, but I've never run into a single kid in the United States who toilet taught herself all by herself. The ones I know all needed a mother or father or grandparent or *somebody* to teach them.

The result of my informal survey of what books on child raising say about toilet teaching is that very few of them do a careful, thoughtful, and comprehensive job on the subject. So where does this leave the poor parent? She can only learn to toilet teach her child the way she learns other aspects of child raising—by trial and error.

As I have pointed out in my own books, toilet teaching is more than teaching the child simply to deposit his BM and urine in a certain special receptacle. It can involve a power struggle between parent and child. It can teach the child that his parents respect his rights as an individual, or it can teach him that his parents are people who push and pressure him regardless of his feelings. Toilet teaching can also produce negative teaching in regard to a child's developing sexual attitudes. (Since the defecatory apparatus and the sexual apparatus are anatomically tied together, negative feelings toward the defecatory organs may unfortunately generalize to the sexual organs as well.)

The interesting part of all this is that toilet teaching is really very simple if you know what to do. The catch is that most parents think they know, but they don't. They need help in learning how. *Parents*™ *Book of Toilet Teaching* is a book that parents have needed for a long time.

Joanna Cole points out that the advice most frequently given to parents about toilet teaching is to relax. But she says she finds this advice to be annoying at worst and useless at best. She says it's like saying "relax" to someone who's about to fly an airplane for the first time. A person who is taking up a plane for the first time will probably be nervous and it won't help her to be told to relax. What will help her is some specific knowledge of how to work the plane and an idea of what to expect when she gets in the air. She also wants an experienced pilot and guide to let her know when she is making a mistake and when she is on the right track. Then she will feel reassured and will be able to relax a bit.

I agree with the author's analysis and I believe she has written the comprehensive kind of book on toilet teaching that will help you as a parent feel confident about toilet teaching your child. One of the main virtues of the book is that it is concrete and down-to-earth. Ms. Cole describes a clear, simple, step-by-step method of toilet teaching your child. As an added gift, in comparison with many child-raising books that are dull, dull, dull, Ms. Cole has written this one in a lively and interesting style.

Ms. Cole not only gives you the information you need, but she gives you a relaxed and comfortable feeling about it all as well. This reassuring attitude toward toilet teaching is conveyed in part by numerous quotes from parents who have toilet taught their children. As you read the book you get the impression you are at a meeting of parents who are sharing their feelings about this subject in a highly supportive fashion.

Ms. Cole herself is a warm, relaxed, and caring person. You feel as if she is saying to you: "I stood in your shoes not so long ago. I worried about how good a job I would be able to do in toilet teaching my child. So I know how you feel right now. But don't worry; everything's going to be all right. I'll tell you what to do and pass on to you the things that other mothers and I have learned, about how to make toilet teaching easier. We had our troubles sometimes, but we came through it and so will you."

The information and reassurance you need is in this book. Read. Relax. Learn. And do a good job and an easygoing job of toilet teaching your child.

# Introduction: What We Know Today About Toilet Teaching

When anthropologists go off to study traditional cultures—for instance, the tribal groups of Africa or the rural villages of the Philippines or the peoples of Indonesia—they often come back to write books about such weighty matters as kinship patterns, religious beliefs, or political structures. But many have taken note as well of more homely subjects like child rearing and baby care. Their reports reveal that babies and young children are often indulged in these societies. Mothers may shrug and laugh and say that toddlers are "too young to understand" or even "unable to learn." Therefore, few demands are put on children until they reach the age of five or six. Since warm climates allow babies to go without clothing (adults simply "hold them out" when they sense a bowel movement or urination coming), and since cleaning up is not a very messy chore in an outdoor

1

setting, toilet teaching is gradual and casual in most traditional cultures. There is no undue stress on perfect performance or rapid learning. In short, the whole business is conducted with a sense of ease and acceptance.

In contrast, toilet teaching in the industrialized countries has until recently been characterized by rigid standards and high expectations. Forty or fifty years ago, it was not unusual for parents to try to "habit train" babies under a year by placing them on the potty at appropriate times. Punishments for lapses were common, and an exaggerated sense of the importance of successes or failures pervaded the atmosphere.

Although there is no one "right" way of toilet teaching, some basic principles are accepted today that were not understood in the past, and these principles are in many ways closer to the style of the preindustrial village than that of the "civilized" nations. It is now generally accepted by child psychologists, for instance, that there is no place for punishment in toilet teaching. Besides being cruel and unfair to the child, punishment fosters a negative self-image and is not effective in producing good toilet habits. In fact, harsh treatment actually slows down toilet learning and is often associated with elimination problems, if not personality disorders, in later life.

It is now also known that early toilet teaching, once considered the duty of a good parent, is not desirable. A toddler cannot learn before he is ready—physically, mentally, and emotionally—and only a minority of children are ready for successful toilet learning before the age of two. One should definitely not try to teach a baby to use the potty.

Although the old methods are still used by some, pediatricians notice a dramatic change in people's thinking. Mothers and fathers today want their children to become confident, outgoing people with strong friendships, loving marriages, and satisfying work. They sense that to foster such personalities in their children, parents must be positive and encouraging, rather than negative and corrective—whether in toilet teaching or any other activity.

The very term "toilet *training*" seems at odds with these humanistic goals, and many child-care writers are replacing it with new words: "toilet learning" for what the child does, and "toilet teaching" for what the parent does. In everyday conversation, these may seem a bit forced at first, but I have adopted them here, as you'll have noticed, for two reasons. First, I do not believe it is possible or desirable to "train" a child like a dog or a horse, and second, I feel that "teaching" and "learning" more accurately describe what goes on in a family when a toddler starts to use the toilet.

In the recent past, as people have become more aware of the harmful effects of the old methods, a few parents have reacted by going to the other extreme. Ironically, they are usually not the ones who would scold a child or punish him for a lapse in control, but they are so wary of putting undue pressure on a toddler that they more or less leave him to learn on his own. This procedure usually doesn't work very well, however, because as most parents realize, toddlers *need* guidance and approval from adults in order to learn new skills and take steps toward independence. So sooner or later these parents find that they have to get involved in their child's toilet learning, whether they want to or not.

They soon discover, as most others have, that there is nothing intimidating about toilet teaching as long as the parents understand a little about how toddlers think (not exactly like their parents!), what techniques have proven

3

effective, and how one's own feelings and attitudes can affect the process. With this information under your belt, you and your toddler can find toilet teaching and toilet learning as simple, natural, and worry-free as "the books" say it should be.

# 1. Don't Start Too Early

Many young parents have heard well-meaning relatives boasting that their babies were "trained by a year" or even earlier. Sometimes the relatives do not stop there, but actually chide the parents of a baby for "neglecting" their child by not initiating toilet teaching early, and some may even offer to teach the child themselves.

One mother told of how her mother-in-law took over the job of "training" her fifteen-month-old when she learned that a second baby was expected. And another parent recalled that a devoted baby-sitter wanted to begin toileting when the baby was only ten months old.

It is best to resist such efforts to pressure you into starting teaching before your child is two years old, since success is much more likely to happen quickly if teaching begins between the ages of two and three. As for a baby under eighteen months, it is definitely not good to try, as it is very unlikely that the baby is physically capable of bladder and bowel control. Those who claim that their babies were "completely trained" under a year certainly do not remember accurately, since it is simply not possible for such young babies to have physical control.

In fact, it has been observed that no matter how early parents begin toilet teaching, children usually end up achieving control at about the same age. Thus, a baby who is started on the potty at fourteen months and another who begins learning at twenty-six months will both have daytime control of bladder and bowel functions at an average age of twenty-eight months. Nighttime dryness will be achieved somewhat later. Starting early, therefore, will only result in a longer period of rushing to the bathroom, cleaning up messes, and feeling frustrated.

In infants, the nerve connections from the brain to the bowel and bladder are not yet established. A newborn baby, therefore, does not experience the sensation of fullness or the urge to push that an adult does. Instead, urination and bowel movements "just happen" without the infant's awareness. These processes are purely involuntary in babies.

As the baby grows, the nerve connections gradually develop, and this development continues throughout childhood, until about age thirteen. Thus, a grade-school child has many neural connections to the bladder and bowel, but not as many as a teenager or an adult. This progressive acquisition of nerve connections explains why younger children still occasionally wet their pants, while most older children and adults rarely do.

A newborn baby is wet most of the time and requires frequent diaper changes because the urine is released often from the bladder. As the baby grows, the bladder begins to retain urine for longer periods, and the urine is released less frequently and in larger amounts. This is a sign that the bladder is maturing.

At the same time, bowel movements will become less frequent and may begin coming at regular, predictable times during the day. Because stools are messier to clean up, parents may attempt to "catch" the movement in the potty, or to "pot" the baby, as this practice is sometimes called. In the days when laundry was done by hand, it was quite understandable that parents would try to reduce the number of soiled diapers, especially when families were large and the amount of domestic work great. In simpler cultures today, where babies often are not diapered at all, families also pot the babies. It may be possible to manage "potting" in a relaxed, no-fault way, but it is much more likely that the practice will lead to trouble. The parent is apt to become overinvolved in the baby's functioning because when potting is successful, it is easy for the parent to assume wrongly that the baby has learned control. That is exactly what happened to the older relatives mentioned earlier, who believed that their babies were "trained" at a year.

In fact, it was the parent—usually the mother in that generation—who was "trained." She may have taught herself to recognize from physical signs when the baby was about to have a bowel movement. Then she quickly took the baby to the bathroom, removed the diaper, and caught the stool in the potty. If the baby was very regular in his movements, the mother learned to set him on the pot at certain times of day. Then she would perch on the edge of the bathtub and entertain the child until the movement was made. In all this, the baby was an innocent bystander. He was not physically or mentally ready to learn control of the bowel, which involves quite a few complicated steps: (1) feeling the urge to defecate; (2) interpreting the sensation to mean "I need to make a bowel movement"; (3) holding the urge; (4) moving to the bathroom, or asking to be taken there; (5) removing clothing, or asking to be undressed; (6) sitting on the potty; and (7) relaxing the sphincter muscles, which releases the stool into the potty.

The baby under eighteen months has not learned any of these steps, but he may learn some other things from the experience of being potted, most of them negative. And what he does learn can contribute to future resistances to toilet learning.

What exactly does the baby learn from being put on the potty too early? He learns that several times a day, for no apparent reason, his mother becomes agitated or abrupt, snatches him up and whisks him to the bathroom. During these times, his mother does not relate to him as a person, but seems attentive to some other thing about him that he cannot comprehend. Only after he has been on the potty for a while does she start acting in her usual way again. Even if the mother's apprehension is not communicated to the child, the experience of being "whisked away" will not add much to the child's sense of order in the world, which contributes to his self-confidence and which is based in large part on his having a positive, fairly predictable, and understandable relationship with the primary adults in his life.

If the baby's bowel movements are regular and the mother anticipates them at certain times of day, the child may learn something else. He learns that several times a day his mother sets him on the potty and waits. She may restrain him from getting up, or she may read to him or otherwise cajole him into staying there. But either way, the baby learns that for some reason he cannot understand, his mother wants and expects him to stay seated, when what he wants to do—if he is a normal, happy baby—is to crawl around or toddle off and see what there is to see in the world. And at this age, he can hardly bear to be restrained from his natural inclinations even for a minute.

Research has shown that children's self-esteem is related to the freedom they are given as babies to move about without restrictions. Thus, strapping an active baby in a stroller for long periods or making efforts to restrain him on the potty is not good for him psychologically.

Some babies learn something else when put on the potty. They become conditioned to move their bowels when they feel the potty seat under them. This learning is very much like the conditioning of Pavlov's famous dogs, who learned to drool when a bell rang. Pavlov, a Russian physiologist, repeatedly put food in the dogs' mouths right after ringing a bell. After a while, the dogs would drool when the bell rang, even if no food was put in their mouths. Their drooling in response to the bell is called a conditioned reflex; it is not voluntary and is not under the animals' control.

The baby who is repeatedly placed on the potty just before a bowel movement learns in a similar way. Whenever she feels the potty under her, she may experience an involuntary stimulation of the bowel and frequently may defecate if there are feces in the rectum. But this response is a conditioned reflex. It does not involve any of the steps needed for control of the bowel mentioned earlier, such as feeling the urge, interpreting the feeling, and holding the urge. The baby is completely passive.

While the parent may avoid some soiled diapers using this conditioning technique, the trouble is that it makes it easy to believe the baby is exercising at least some amount of control. A child who has regular movements and who is conditioned to defecate when put on the potty appears to be "going to the potty" quite successfully. When mother praises her for going, the baby will smile back, pleased at her parent's attention. It may seem as if the baby knows what's going on. The parent thinks that the baby is "on the way" to being "trained" and begins to have some expectations. It is inevitable that these expectations will be communicated to the child, if not directly then surely by indirect emotional reactions.

A parent's expectations for a child, when they are child-centered and based on what the child is capable of when he is capable of it, are a positive force for growth and self-reliance. But when parents expect too much of a child at a given developmental stage, when the child simply cannot, no matter what he does, fulfill the parents' expectations, then failure is built into the situation. And setting it up so that a happy, bouncing baby will experience early frustration and failure is surely not what we want for our children.

Failure will happen with the baby who is potted early because babies go through changes as they grow. Patterns of sleeping, eating, and eliminating can change drastically from one month to another. Thus, a baby who has regular bowel movements at ten months may become very irregular by fourteen months. Suddenly the "good" baby is having no success at all on the potty. Mother thinks baby is backsliding, forgetting what he has learned. Of course, baby hasn't forgotten. He hasn't learned anything in the first place, but mother doesn't realize this. She expresses irritation, directly or indirectly. The baby cannot say, "Look, Mother, I don't really have control over my bowels yet." He cannot even say, "I can't help it. I didn't do it on purpose," because he isn't even aware of what's happening with the diapers and the potty. And if he were, he wouldn't be able to articulate such subtle feelings.

What he can and will do is respond to his mother's frustration and anger. He will frown and look angry himself, perhaps have a tantrum. Or he may withdraw emotionally from an unpleasant situation and busy himself with something else. These perfectly natural reactions may seem like acts of defiance to the parent, who expects the baby to feel sorry for the "mistake."

There's a communication gap between baby and parent in these situations, and it is not surprising that some parents who expect too much from babies resort to scoldings and punishment. Even those parents who keep the lid on their tempers often report that they feel sorely tried and tempted, especially when there is pressure from others to teach the child at an early age.

So here is yet another lesson the baby learns from too early teaching. He learns to associate the potty with parental expectations that he cannot meet or even comprehend, and with equally unexplained parental anger, if not shaming and punishment. These lessons will not work toward making toileting a purely positive experience when the time comes for real learning. In fact, studies have shown that the earlier and the more severe toilet teaching is, the more likelihood there is for problems with elimination later on.

When the child gets acquainted with the potty closer to the time when she will be ready to learn, then she will have only positive associations with it. The potty will mean that she is getting big, ready to grow up a bit and be like her parents, older siblings, and other important people in her life. She is less likely to resist learning to use the potty in these circumstances, especially if she has had ample opportunities to be "babied" when she was a baby. Indeed, research shows that children who have had their dependency needs met adequately as babies are more likely to be independent as they grow older. Almost paradoxically, babies who are pushed to be self-reliant too soon tend to be more clinging and less willing to move out on their own.

One opportunity for showing care and love to a baby is

at changing time. Some parents see diaper changing as a necessary inconvenience and cost, and eagerly look forward to the time when the baby will be out of diapers. In families that have real money problems or many children, there may be some reason to give in to the temptation to try teaching toileting early. But even under these circumstances, many families think of the baby's interests first.

They think of changing time as a social experience between parent and baby, a quiet time for talking or singing songs. Of course, the older baby will be restless on the dressing table, which is even more reason for making changing time a social time. One parent remembered, "I used to put a selection of little toys and objects, even small books, on the dressing table, which my baby would study while I changed her. We would talk about the pictures in the books or make up rhymes about the toys, and before you knew it, the diaper was changed. Overall, it was a pleasant experience for both of us, although I remember saying this to someone and having her look at me in disbelief. I guess the idea of diaper changing being pleasant is hard to accept for someone who isn't a parent."

By changing the diaper in a caring way, you are fulfilling your baby's needs for dependency, closeness, and unconditional acceptance. You are showing her that you love her and that everything about her person, including the products of her body, are acceptable to you. To keep this message clear, it's best not to say "icky-poo" or "stinky-pants" even in a joking way when changing a diaper. It may seem harmless and even loving, depending on how it is said, but it is a double message nonetheless, and the baby takes in the negative part with the positive.

By trying to catch the bowel movement in the potty instead of changing the diaper, the parent may communicate to the baby that the feces are unpleasant and that the mother or father does not like to touch them. It would be a natural association for the child to feel rejected on some level by this perception, and child psychologists point out that since the organs of excretion happen to be close to the genitals, sending a message that the feces are disgusting may cause feelings of shame and guilt associated with sex. These feelings can persist throughout life.

Early efforts to teach the baby to use the potty can also make toileting an arena for battles of will between parents and child. The parents communicate that they want him very much to use the potty. This gives the child a powerful weapon in any struggle to assert himself, because unlike other areas of struggle, he's the only one who can make the bowel movement. The parents can wash the child's hair, put on the snowsuit, take away harmful objects, strap him into a car seat. And the baby really has no choice but to do the parents' will, because the parents are bigger and stronger. But once the child gains control, she can withhold a bowel movement from the potty, and the parents, as big and strong as they may be, are helpless. The child may experience the parents as pushing and pressuring her and also as being intrusive, trying to control that which should belong to the child alone, her body. The parent-child relationship can become characterized by a pattern of pressure and cajoling on the parents' part, and reactive stubbornness and withholding, or constipation, on the child's. Giving enemas or using suppositories may be experienced as more intrusion and will only intensify the child's withholding behavior.

Although it is not known whether toilet-teaching procedures in and of themselves can cause personality problems, it is clearly undesirable to get into a struggle of wills over a natural body function, and such a struggle is much more likely to start if toilet teaching is begun too early. Waiting until the child is ready—physically, emotionally, and mentally—can make toilet learning the child's own accomplishment, achieved with the parents' help, not their pressuring. Such an experience fosters pride in both the parents and the child, and lays the groundwork for a relationship based on mutual trust and respect.

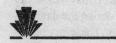

# 2. When Is a Toddler Ready?

Between twenty and thirty months, parents may begin to notice signs of readiness for toilet learning in their toddlers. Tradition has it that girls are usually ahead of boys, and statistics support the conventional wisdom. In everyday experience, however, parents find that many boys are early and some girls are late. Parents of a set of boy-girl twins, for instance, reported that, to their surprise, it was the boy who learned to use the toilet first while his sister wasn't ready until several months later.

Bowel control usually comes before bladder control, although again there are exceptions to the rule. The sequence of readiness typically follows this order: first, nighttime bowel control; then, daytime bowel control; next, daytime bladder control; and finally, nighttime bladder control.

Physical signs to watch for that indicate a readiness for

daytime bowel control may include: regularity in bowel movements; pausing in play when having a movement; making sounds and grimaces and getting red in the face or even crying when defecating. These signs show that the action is becoming more voluntary and the child is more aware of it than previously.

Signs of readiness for bladder control may be: a dry diaper for an hour or two or even longer during the daytime, and an occasional dry diaper after a nap. These periods of dryness are evidence that the bladder is maturing and holding urine for a longer time.

Accompanying these physical signs are signals that the child's awareness is developing also. Some children will ask to be changed when the diaper is wet or soiled. Others may simply cry or complain. And some may just announce "poopy" and point to the diaper. All of these reactions show that the child knows she has urinated or made a BM.

The next step is for the child to anticipate the action. One mother said, "He first started to be aware of when he was going to have a BM at about twenty-eight months. He would tell me and then go ahead and do it." This stage shows true readiness for control because the child is physically and mentally able to understand and anticipate a bowel movement. Compare this response with a parent's description of a child who is not yet aware: "When we first got the potty and he was trying to do bowel movements in it, he would sit for a while, then get up and turn around to see if he'd done anything. He kept getting up to look—it was so cute we took a picture of him. I don't think he physically realized when he'd made a BM."

It's hard for most parents to realize that a young toddler may be mentally unaware of the process of elimination and may not make the connection between the sensations of urinating and defecating and the presence of wetness and stools. Often the bulky diaper prevents a child from making the association and sometimes parents find that leaving the diaper off for a period of time helps.

Other signs of readiness that usually occur between the ages of two and three are emotional and maturational. At this age, many toddlers develop quite an interest in cleanliness and neatness, sometimes to the point of obsession. A child may cry and become agitated if a toy or piece of clothing gets dirty, or even reprimand her parents for being messy if something is out of order. At this age, too, toddlers like to help with housework, especially putting things away and cleaning and shining furniture. In his classic book *Baby and Child Care*, Dr. Benjamin Spock says, "... the preference for cleanliness that a child gains at around two years ... is actually the foundation for a lifelong preference for unsticky hands, for clean clothes, for a neat home, for an orderly way of doing business." Parents can encourage this sense of orderliness in their children, and one way of doing this is by seeing it as a sign of readiness for toilet learning.

Another sign of emotional readiness is the toddler's increasing self-awareness, especially her own sense that she is growing up. One child may insist loudly that she is "*not* a baby" while another may enjoy pointing out the differences between babies and big boys like himself. Almost all two-year-olds want to do the same things as their parents and older children, and this eagerness to take part in the grown-up world may include using the toilet.

The signs of physical, mental, and emotional readiness develop gradually, and they may not all be present at once. Emotional readiness can fluctuate considerably, as every parent knows: a child may want to be a big girl one day and the next may insist on being treated like a baby. In addition to such everyday mood swings, stressful situations such as the arrival of a new baby, a move, even a visit from grandparents may bring babyish behavior to the fore for a while.

In a particular child, moreover, some signs of readiness may simply not appear. In fact, when parents talk about this period in their toddlers' lives, they often mention that their children did not do what the books said they were "supposed" to do. One mother said, "I kept reading about waiting until she was dry for long periods. But Alison was *never* dry. She was a big drinker and a big wetter right up until the time she learned to use the toilet. If I had paid attention to the books, I never would have believed she could have learned."

Another parent said, "Gregory never went through that fastidious period they are supposed to have, and he still couldn't care less if he's wet or not. He's come home from nursery school having had an accident in clothes that dry fast and not said anything to me. The only way I've known is because his shoes are wet!"

"My boys had a lot of colds, which gave them diarrhea," said another parent, "so they were never regular at all."

And yet all these children did learn to use the potty before they were three.

Knowing that bowel readiness usually comes before bladder, many parents begin teaching their toddlers to use the potty for BMs before the second birthday. Indeed, this procedure seems to be the method of toilet teaching traditionally recommended. The child is taken to the potty at regular times, usually after breakfast, for a bowel movement. At other times, however, he still wears a diaper.

The mother of a nineteen-month-old described how she began this method: "A few weeks ago, Kathy indicated that her diaper was dirty and she didn't like it. So I told her she could go on the potty, and she sat there. At first, she would not do a BM. She would get up and I'd put the diaper back on, and *then* she would do it. But the other morning she decided to do it on the potty. So now I'm setting up a regular schedule. First thing in the morning, I tell her to go and sit there, and she doesn't dilly-dally. She goes, she does it, good-bye!"

For this mother and daughter, such an arrangement seems easy and efficient, but other parents see this approach as making more trouble than it saves. The child has to be taught twice—first for bowel control and later for bladder. The procedure extends the learning period, and since diapers have to be removed for bowel movements, the child can't learn to pull down her own pants. Many parents feel that waiting until later is more comfortable. The learning period is shorter and the child can assume responsibility for complete toileting in one step.

Many parents find that their children are ready for bladder and bowel control at two and a half or before. Others find that their children aren't ready until after two and a half. And still others feel that toilet learning might be possible for their toddlers before two and a half, but that they are *just* ready, and control is imperfect. These parents seem to feel, Why bother now? It will be such a hassle. Let's just wait a bit.

One such parent said, "A friend of mine has a lot of contact with children and she's a very good observer. She mentioned that parents often say their two-year-olds are 'perfectly trained,' but the kids seem to have accidents *all* the time. Since she said that, I've been watching at Mark's day-care center, and I see the same thing. The kids are in underpants at two years three months, but every day they take home wet clothing in a plastic bag." This mother decided to wait and didn't initiate toilet teaching until Mark was two years ten months. "I didn't want to pressure him.

We got a potty when he was twenty-six months old and he was very interested. He wanted to sit on it and he was kind of pleased one time when something came out. And then the interest faded very quickly. You know, the new toy wasn't new anymore. And at that point, I didn't care. I thought I'd be just as happy having him stay in diapers for a while. It was easy to take along diapers when we went out and I didn't have the problem of trying to find a bathroom when he had to go."

Another mother whose son was in diapers until almost three agreed. "When they are younger," she said, "it often seems as if it's the parents who are trained and not the children. The parents keep reminding the kids about going to the bathroom and they're always saying 'Let's go to the potty now.' It really is a lot of trouble."

Judging from these parents' impressions, it may seem that the definition of "ready" can depend on how much time you want to spend in the bathroom—and on the way there.

Dr. T. Berry Brazelton, the well-known pediatrician and author, made a study of 1,170 children over a period of ten years. Using a no-pressure technique of toilet teaching recommended by Dr. Brazelton, parents reported that 80 percent of the children had achieved daytime bladder and bowel control between the ages of two and two and a half, with control meaning no more than one accident per week.

Reading these figures, a parent might well assume that his child *should* have control by two and a half. Looked at another way, however, the statistics show that fully 20 percent of these normal children had *not* learned by this age. In fact, out of the total 1,170 children, 150 did not complete the learning process until three and a half, and 108 were not in control until age four. Yet Dr. Brazelton and the parents considered these late bloomers perfectly normal and did not treat them as "problem cases." Eventually, they learned when they were ready.

Although most parents have read about the age range for normal readiness, many can't help feeling confused and concerned when their own children are later than average. One mother whose daughter was not yet using the potty at thirty-five months said, "My child is going to be the oldest living human in diapers!" Other parents try to reassure themselves and others by adopting a relaxed attitude, but this is not always so easy when your child is the only one of your acquaintance who is late.

The mother of the boy who kept getting up to look in the potty for BMs said, "Kevin was in a play group with two girls and two boys, and when they were about two and a half, they were all trained—all of them except Kevin. I used to watch them and think that he should probably be trained, too. Everyone else was. But he really wasn't ready. He wasn't dry and I just didn't think he had the control. Then one day when he was just shy of three, he said, 'I want to start wearing underpants.' It took about a week or two before he was fully trained. He practically did it by himself when he was finally ready."

The differences among children are shown in the example of a set of fraternal twins, David and Paul. David paid no attention to the potties when they were purchased shortly before the second birthday. Paul, however, would sit on one of the potties and try to make a BM.

"David would come with his clothes on and sit next to Paul and be very interested in what was going on," said the twins' mother. "He had no interest in doing it himself. But he was thrilled for Paul, and whenever Paul did anything, they both got very excited. It was very funny and very cute. They would look in the potty and check out what Paul had done." By thirty-one months, Paul was wearing underpants all the time, but David still wasn't interested in toilet learning. "He wouldn't even try during all those months that Paul was learning," continued his mother. Even after Paul had been in underpants for several months, David still didn't show any interest.

"I sort of resigned myself to the fact that we didn't seem to be getting anywhere and I went back to buying the large box of diapers instead of the little one. The day after I'd bought a big box, I said to David, 'Do you want to try going to the potty?' and he said, 'Sure.' And he went. In two days, he was in underpants and there was never a problem after that."

The twins' story shows how readiness can be a matter of learning style—*how* a child learns a new skill—rather than a purely physical matter. Some children like to take things in stages, practice a bit, learn by trial and error. Others like to wait until they're good and ready.

"Good and ready." This phrase, rather than "only just ready," seems to describe how many of today's parents are looking at toilet teaching. They seem willing to read the child rather than the book, as one mother put it, and follow the child's lead. Parents often say that when they waited until the child started the proceedings by asking to use the potty or wear pants the learning was rapid and painless.

However, watching the child and following her lead is not the same thing as doing nothing. The parents should definitely *not* be passive in the process. Your child looks to you for confidence in her ability to succeed and for guidance in learning a new skill. Preparing your child for toilet learning is essential and you can do this by teaching her to recognize her own body signals, showing her what the toilet is for, and letting her know how to use it. Some parents are so afraid of putting undue pressure on their toddler that they don't tell her their expectations. They never communicate clearly that they expect her to learn to use the toilet like everybody else, and because of their own over-concern about pressure, they may fail to respond to readiness cues from the child.

Once a child expresses, directly or indirectly, the desire to use the potty, parents should pick up on the idea. Ignoring the child's signals—perhaps because you are too busy at that period to pay attention—may send the message that you lack confidence in him. A three-year-old who said, "I'm not a big boy because I still wear diapers" was indirectly asking his parents if they considered him capable of being a big boy. Perhaps he hesitated to say directly, "I want to use the potty now" or "I want to wear underpants" because he wasn't sure whether his parents had confidence in him. When the parents picked up on the cue and encouraged him to trade in his diaper for pants, he learned almost at once and, according to his mother, "He just beamed!"

When parents show a child that they understand where he is and accept him where he is, and when they offer their support when he is ready to grow and learn, they are encouraging his autonomy—whether he's a late bloomer or an early one.

# 3. Preparing Your Child for Toilet Learning

Once you have noticed some or all of the signs of readiness described in the previous chapter, and your child is approaching his second birthday, you will want to start preparing him for using the toilet. You will want to assume the role of a gentle teacher. Your job is to help him master a new skill, and the best way to think of the process is to compare it to learning to walk or ride a bike. The child is the active learner; he may take a few steps today and crawl a bit after taking a fall; he may wobble, but he'll still want to proceed at his own rate. You come in when he needs guidance or assistance. Your attitude of calm encouragement will be the best help he can get.

In preparing your child for using the toilet, you will want to teach her a few basic facts about her body and about the toilet. For instance, you'll want her to learn to recognize (and gradually anticipate) when she is having a bowel movement or urinating; to inform you when she is about to go; to understand what the toilet is for; to learn to sit on the potty; and to practice urinating and defecating in the potty. These are things you can casually teach her over a period of time in the course of your everyday life together before she may be ready for consistent, all-day control.

*Recognizing and understanding physical sensations*: When your child is about eighteen months old, you can help her recognize when she is having a bowel movement. When you see her straining, you can say matter-of-factly, "Janie is making a BM." If she urinates when the diaper is off, you can take advantage of the situation by saying, "Janie is making peepee." In this way, you're teaching her that urine and feces come from her body, and you're forming an association between her bodily sensations and the presence of a wet or soiled diaper.

It will take a while for your child to develop the ability to anticipate a bowel movement. She may begin by telling you that she *has had* a BM; later inform you when she *is having* one; and finally let you know when she *is about to have* one. (This same sequence will hold true for urination a bit later in her development.)

Parents sometimes expect a child to know that she "should" go in the potty and scold her for announcing that she is going in her diaper. At this stage, however, praising her for the announcement is more effective because it encourages her to increase her awareness of her bodily sensations.

Not every child, however, will want to communicate with her parents about her elimination patterns. If yours doesn't feel like chatting, don't worry. As long as you have mentioned the connections to her a few times in a friendly way, you can assume that she has gotten the idea and will be able to make use of it when the time comes.

*Learning a new vocabulary*: When you teach your toddler to recognize the sensations of elimination, you are also adding some important new words to his vocabulary, so you should decide which ones are most acceptable to you and your family. Some families are comfortable with the "correct" terms: *urinate* and *have a bowel movement* or *BM*. Others feel that these are too cold for everyday use or too difficult for a young child to say. Words like *peepee*, *tinkle*, *weewee*, *sis*, *caca*, *poopy*, *poops*, and *duty* may seem friendlier and easier for little children to understand. We adults may have forgotten all about these words, but they begin to reappear in our lives as our children start to use the potty. It's a good idea to choose words that will be appropriate not only in your home, but in those of your neighbors and relatives as well. One sophisticated and respectable professional woman, who had come of age in the sixties, said she had made a big mistake in using words at home that were definitely *not* acceptable for her two-year-old to pipe up with on a bus or during a visit with grandma. In your search for inoffensive terms, however, please realize that you probably won't get away with a euphemism like "going to the bathroom." It will be taken quite literally by a two- or three-year-old. If you mean urinate, you'll have to come right out and say it.

*Observing and imitating others*: While your child is learning about his own body and its processes of elimination, he will also be learning what the toilet is and what it is for. The best way to learn is to see others using it. Most parents today are quite free about letting babies and toddlers join them in the bathroom. Indeed, there is a certain stage of babyhood when it is hard for a parent to get away; it's so difficult for the baby to let you out of her sight that it may be next to impossible to take a bath or go to the toilet without having her along.

For a boy, social contact in the bathroom with his father can be motivation for learning. One father said, "There's far more incentive for a little boy to urinate with his father than alone. If you have the opportunity to do it with somebody else, that's terrific."

Another father described the frankly imitative behavior of his son this way: "Sometimes I'll be on the toilet reading, and Peter will come in, get a magazine, and sit down on his potty and 'read' too."

Not every parent, of course, is willing to open the bathroom door to his child. Some parents are modest—they want their privacy, and there isn't anything wrong with this, as long as there are plenty of other opportunities for the child to observe people using the toilet. Older siblings, neighbors' children, or older children in a playgroup are ideal role models, and the desire to imitate them may be even stronger than the desire to imitate parents.

People often report touching scenes between brothers and sisters in which the older child takes on a teaching role with the younger. One parent described the following relationship between siblings: "It was wonderful how supportive Stephen—the older one—was of Peter's toilet learning. He would get so excited about Peter's performance on the potty. He would call us in to look and he would sit with Peter when he was going. And if Stephen had to go himself, he would say, 'Peter, come with me. You can sit on your potty.'

"It was quite amazing because Stephen is often jealous

of things that Peter does. Yet there he was encouraging Peter and sharing the experience with him."

In other cases, a younger child encouraged the older: "When John was learning and Karen was about a year old, she was like a little cheerleading section, just standing there and sort of rooting for him."

And parents of children at a day-care center for infants and toddlers noticed with some amusement that the bathroom, with its several potties, was a popular gathering place for the toddlers—they were intensely interested in what each one had produced in the potty.

This kind of mutual encouragement among young children explains why a second child is proverbially said to learn toileting more easily than a first child, and why in some traditional cultures parents take no part in toilet teaching at all. Toddlers are told to watch the older children and do as they do.

*Mention the advantages*: Another way to prepare young toddlers for toilet learning is to point out the advantages of giving up the diaper. For instance, one toddler who was troubled by painful diaper rashes was reassured once or twice by his father, "When you get bigger and use the potty instead of diapers, you won't get such bad rashes."

Another child resisted diaper changes because they interrupted his play. His mother reported, "When he protested, I would sometimes say, 'When you're able to go to the potty, then I won't have to do this. I could just wipe you.' I think I was trying subconsciously to plant a seed—the idea that life would become easier and more comfortable when he started using the potty."

Most toddlers don't seem to mind wearing a wet or dirty diaper, and the preference for being clean eventually comes from the influence of others. After changing a diaper, you might occasionally say, "There, now you're all clean and dry again. Doesn't that feel nice?" It will also help to change your toddler frequently, so he won't get accustomed to feeling wet.

Another incentive can be to mention occasionally that the child will one day wear underpants and use the potty like an older sibling or friend. Be sure, however, to present these ideas in a moderate tone and to keep them *infrequent*. The point is to "plant a seed," not to convince the child that he should give up diapers right now. Don't expect a positive reaction or even any reaction. A toddler will often respond to such remarks as if he hasn't even heard them. Fine. Trust that the seed has been planted and that it will sprout at the appropriate time.

*Children's books about the potty*: All of these lessons can be clarified and reinforced by reading your child one of the several good books available on toilet learning (listed below). My favorite is a paperback called *No More Diapers!* by Joae Graham Brooks, M.D., and members of the staff of the Boston Children's Medical Center. It's a three-part book: part one is for the parents and presents general information on toilet teaching; part two is an illustrated story for toddlers about a little boy who gives up diapers and gets his own potty; part three tells essentially the same story, only this time the main character is a little girl.

Some parents say they find this sort of book a little silly. But you may be surprised at how important such a story can be for your child. It may even be his favorite for a time, one that he'll want read to him several times a day. As tedious as these repeated readings can be for the adult, you can find encouragement in your toddler's interest, which is sure evidence of his motivation to grow into this new skill himself.

There are several reasons why a toddler will take a book like *No More Diapers!* so seriously. The first and most obvious is that it deals with a developmental step that is crucial in his life right now. It also shows a model for each sex to identify with, and provides much needed information about what the toilet and potty are for. And it spells out *exactly* what is expected of the child who is listening to the story.

Another good function of the book is that it takes some of the burden of toilet teaching off the parents, which can make things easier for both the parents and the child. While a two-year-old wants to please his parents, he doesn't want to please them *too* much. He has to keep some part of himself separate in order to gain autonomy, to be his own person. So finding out about using the toilet from a third party, be it an older child or a book, can help minimize parent-child conflicts over this sensitive issue.

The book will serve different purposes at different stages, and the child's interest in it will wax and wane accordingly. At first, the book will be a source of new information. Later, when the child is actually giving up the diaper in exchange for underpants, it will serve as a reassuring review of what is happening. And after the child has learned to use the potty, he may still like to come back to the book occasionally to consolidate the experience in his mind and to get a sense of how far he's come. I recently saw a boy and a girl, who had both been in underpants for at least two years, come across a copy of *No More Diapers!* at a home they were visiting. There was instant, tacit agreement between them. Moving in unison, they carried the book to the nearest adult and settled in for a trip down memory lane.

Here is a listing of a few good books to read to children about toilet learning:

*No More Diapers!* by Joae Graham Brooks, M.D., and members of the staff of the Boston Children's Medical Center. Delacorte Press/Seymour Lawrence. 1971. Paperback. $5.95.

*Once Upon a Potty* by Alona Frankel. Barron's. 1980. Board covers. $3.95.

*Toilet Learning: The Picture Book Technique for Children and Parents* by Alison Mack. Little, Brown and Company. 1978. Hardcover. $8.95.

*Getting a potty*: A few months before you think your child may be ready, you will want to buy a potty. You can choose a seat that fits on the big toilet or a potty chair that sits on the floor. Most parents and pediatricians recommend the potty on the floor for several reasons: the child will feel more secure with her feet on the floor; there will be less chance of the child's getting frightened by almost falling in or off; and the little potty is her own special possession, which can increase her motivation to use it. Some children, however, prefer a seat on the big toilet, and if this is the case with your child, be sure to provide a sturdy stepping stool.

Many potties come with detachable deflectors, or plastic guards, for boys to keep urine from spraying around the room. Most child-care experts recommend that the deflector not be used because little boys tend to hurt themselves on it and the experience may make them shy of the potty after that. Anyway, a boy soon learns to hold his penis down because it is fun to aim into the pot and hear the noise. (A boy will have to urinate sitting down on the potty or there will be too much splashing. When he wants to stand, he can use the big toilet.)

Many potties also come with trays for snacks and toys. A tray is fine unless it is used to restrain a child on the potty against his will. Generally speaking, it's a good idea to remove the tray so the child will have free and easy access to the potty.

There are also potties that play a tune when urine and feces fall into them. The purpose is to help a toddler learn when he has produced something. I've heard, however, that children soon learn that they can make the potty play its music by dropping toys and other objects into it.

Some potties also have lids, which can be useful for keeping the family dog from investigating what may be inside!

Basically, it doesn't matter which style you choose, as long as the potty sits solidly on the floor without tipping, has no sharp edges or points, and has a pot that can be easily removed.

*Introduce the potty gradually*: At first, simply show the potty to your child, explain what it is, and tell her that it belongs to her alone. Say that when she stops wearing diapers and starts wearing big-girl pants, this is where she will go when she has to urinate or have a BM.

Most people put the potty on the bathroom floor next to the toilet. This spot makes it clear that the potty is the child's toilet and reinforces the information you have given her about what the potty is for.

Let her explore the potty, play with it, and sit on it with her clothes on. Don't insist at first that she take off the diaper and sit, and don't suggest that she actually use the potty yet. The idea of using the potty may be initially frightening or at least a little foreign. For a toddler, the diaper is familiar, reassuring, and warm. A soiled diaper probably doesn't feel cold and clammy as an adult may imagine; no doubt it is kept warm by body heat. In contrast, the potty seat will feel cold and strange to a little child.

Wait a few days or a week until she is thoroughly accustomed to the new piece of furniture before asking if she would like to sit on it without her diaper. Then choose a time when she may be about to have a BM. If the potty is cold and she protests, let her get up; it may help, however, to say that the seat will warm up if she sits on it for a minute. Ask her to try and see what happens. The idea of an experiment may appeal to her. One mother said she suggested this to her two-year-old shortly after they had read *Goldilocks and the Three Bears*, and she was charmed to hear the little girl say, after the potty was sufficiently warm, "It's not too cold, it's not too hot, it's just right!"

*A word about praise*: When your child does produce feces or urine in the potty, she will probably be delighted and you will share her excitement. Praise her, give her a hug. But don't overdo it. It's her accomplishment, and too much praise changes a natural learning process into a performance for her parents. Overpraise may also make her wonder if you think she needs excessive encouragement to get on with the ordinary business of growing up, or if your disappointment in future failures will be proportional to your present enthusiasm. So making a big fuss every time she uses the potty both steals her thunder and puts pressure on her. It's best to tone down your reactions. A warm smile and a simple comment like "fine" or "good" will serve nicely.

*Don't flush right away*: It is recommended that parents *not* flush away the first bowel movements or urine while the child is still in the bathroom. One reason for this precaution is that the toddler does not share the adult's practical attitude toward feces as something to be disposed of. A toddler's thinking is still at the magical stage—she may see the products of her body as a precious part of herself. As such, they are fascinating, even beautiful. One little girl confided to her mother, "I think my poops are pretty." A child at this stage may be bewildered and even offended if you first praise her for producing a BM and then get rid of it as quickly as possible.

The mother of a three-year-old described her son's early reaction to having bowel movements in the potty like this: "For about the first two weeks, Peter was proud of his BMs. He would invite us to come and look, and he would be reluctant to have them flushed away. He wanted to save them. So I would just wait until he was doing something else."

Another reason to be careful about flushing at first is because it is not uncommon for young toddlers to have unexpressed fears of the toilet. The noise of flushing, the chance of falling in, the sight of the feces being "swallowed up"—all of these can frighten a little child and may cause him to avoid using the potty for months afterward. If your child seems to be afraid of the toilet, see chapter 7 for ways of diminishing the fear.

If, on the other hand, your child is not one of the fearful, and seems to enjoy the toilet, encourage her to learn to flush by herself.

*Developing a daily routine, or not*: Once the child has become comfortable with the potty, traditional advice is to establish a daily routine to encourage regularity in bowel movements. Start taking the child to the potty once a day, preferably after breakfast, this advice says, but observe the child's own schedule and be flexible. If he usually has a

BM after lunch, don't be rigid about the after-breakfast notion. While he is sitting, give him a cookie, read to him, or let him play with a toy. It might even work to play a music box as a timer; when the time is over, the child gets up. In any case, don't keep him there for more than five or ten minutes, and never, never restrain him on the seat. The child shouldn't be scolded if he wants to get up, nor punished if he does, nor should he be pressured to produce a BM. If the child does have a bowel movement or urinates, praise him mildly, remembering not to overdo it. Limit the routine to once, or at most twice, a day.

If your toddler is fairly regular to begin with, and has a calm, compliant personality, the daily routine may work easily for you. Even if it does, however, it is still wise to keep the following cautions in mind: the child who goes happily to the potty every morning for a while may suddenly stop being so regular, or may suddenly say "no" and really mean it. If this happens, you may feel bewildered, disappointed, and annoyed, but keep in mind that toilet teaching should never become mired in a battle of wills. Drop the routine for that day and for a week or so after. If you like having a routine, begin it again later, but do discontinue it whenever resistance develops. The idea is to encourage regularity, not to create an aversion to the routine.

Despite the fact that the daily routine is recommended in most child-care books—*How to Parent* by Dr. Fitzhugh Dodson is a notable and refreshing exception—it seems that few parents use it. In the first place, toddlers are often not regular at all, so setting them on the potty at a certain time is quite useless. In the second place, many children are not likely to go off placidly for potty drill just because their parents think it is time to go. Indeed, they may resist for that very reason. I did not use the daily routine with my child, and I have always felt that if I had, the proverbial struggle of wills would have developed almost immediately. I also suspect that most cases of the "battle of the bowel" could have been avoided if parents had not been trying so hard to follow the instructions in the books.

Instead of a daily routine, many parents prefer to follow the child's bodily signals. If they notice that she is about to have a BM, they may suggest trying to use the potty. Or if she says she has to go, they will take her to the bathroom. And there is no doubt that many, many children have learned to use the toilet perfectly well without a daily routine.

What you decide may largely depend on your own family preferences and your own bathroom habits. Some people are regular and keep track of bowel movements. Others don't pay much attention. Some never stay long in the bathroom; they wait until the urge is strong, go in, do their business, and get out. Others like to get some good reading matter, settle down, and spend some time on the toilet. So while a child-care book may recommend against reading to a child on the potty because it might distract him, your child may find it natural to imitate your literary style, and he may *need* a little distraction to help him relax.

The important thing is that the atmosphere in the bathroom—whether you go there on demand or on schedule—should be peaceful, not rushed or tense. A child should learn from his parents' example that, however urgent or interesting other activities are, one's bodily needs are important too. This is the attitude that will help develop good bathroom habits.

*More potty practice*: Some parents recommend another kind of potty practice, which I'll call the no-diaper-with-potty-nearby session. The purpose of this exercise is a little different from the daily routine. Rather than encouraging regularity, the no-diaper session provides a relaxed opportunity to practice control.

The child is left bare from the waist down (in warm surroundings, of course) and the potty is placed conveniently nearby. You can do this in the kitchen, in the child's room, or even in the backyard. And you can do it every day or just once in a while. You say, "The potty is here if you need it to make pee-pee or a BM." Be prepared to mop up puddles and be neutral about them, and praise successes moderately. When the play period is over, put the diaper on again and return the potty to its original place in the bathroom.

*What the preparation period is and is not*: The preparation period is a time for becoming comfortable with the potty and with the idea of using it. It is a time for practicing urinating and having bowel movements in the potty, as often or as infrequently as the child wishes. The preparation period is not the actual learning period, when the child has given up diapers and is in the process of mastering the ability to remain clean and dry all the time.

During the preparation period, it isn't necessary or even desirable to put the child in training pants (see chapter 4 for more about pants) or to communicate the expectation that he will have every BM in the potty. There should be no disappointment if the child has an "accident," since "accidents" are the norm for this period. The child is getting used to the idea of toileting. That's all.

The preparation period will last for as long or as short a time as is necessary for the individual child. Some children will make all their BMs in the potty at nineteen or twenty months, and a few months later will be asking to have their diapers taken off when they have to urinate. Other children will sit on the potty once or twice when it is first introduced, perhaps urinate in it or have a BM, then totally ignore it for six months. Still others will alternate between periods of intense interest and lack of it.

You should not be worried about your child's learning style. That is her concern. Your concern during the preparation period is simply to make sure you've done your part. And that is to teach your child the basics of toileting. You'll have told him that urine and feces come from his body; you'll have taught him the words you want him to use for bathroom functions; and you'll have helped him recognize and interpret the bodily signals associated with elimination. You'll have helped him find out what the toilet is for by letting him observe others using it, and you'll have given him a gentle introduction to his own potty and helped him practice on it. And finally, you'll have let him know your confident expectation that when he is big enough, he will wear underpants and use the toilet just like the older children and adults he knows.

This is all that is necessary. Even if your child seems content to stay in diapers forever, you can relax because you know that your job at this stage has been done. Trust that all the information is there inside that little head, even if your child seems to have forgotten it. When readiness is complete—physical and emotional—you'll see that it is all there, waiting to unfold. The next chapter will tell you how to proceed when this happens and the preparation period gives way to the learning period.

# 4. No More Daytime Diaper: Step by Step

After your child has shown signs of readiness and has been amply prepared for toilet learning, you may be pleasantly surprised one day to hear her say, "I don't want to wear diapers anymore. I want to use the potty like a big girl."

If this happens, strike while the iron is hot. Do not ignore the request. Plan a time with your child to go shopping for underpants. If it's convenient that day, you might say, "Fine. We'll go to the store after your nap and get you some big-girl underpants." If it's a hectic day, just set a date for another time, and keep it. Then follow the step-by-step guide given later in this chapter for making the switch from diapers to pants.

But what should you do if your child does not express a wish to give up diapers? What about the toddler who "couldn't care less"? His second birthday passes, one month

**41**

follows another, and he never says, "I'm ready." In fact, he seems blissfully unaware that he "ought" to be interested. He doesn't pick up any of the tactful hints you drop, and you wonder if he'll be going off to high school in his diapers.

One often recommended solution to a problem like this is: don't treat it as a problem. Wait it out until the child decides, even if the child is three or almost four. Those who recommend this approach feel strongly that leaving the decision to the child both fosters autonomy and results in fewer conflicts and problems during the learning period. Some of the parents already quoted have used this advice successfully, and if the approach appeals to you, you can follow it easily. Simply continue to use the suggestions in the previous chapter for preparing for toilet learning, continue to suggest to your child that he might like to use the potty, and continue to allow him to experiment in his own way. When he does express the wish to give up diapers, you can move ahead. If he seems to be dropping hints that he would like to, you might ask directly, "Would you like to switch to underpants now? I think you can handle it if you want to." If he says yes, you're on the way.

Many parents, however, may not be willing to wait. They feel their child is ready and may get impatient thinking of all those diapers they'll have to change before the child decides to say those magic words. They reason that if the child is ready and is showing he's ready in every way except a direct statement, there is no reason the parents can't take the first step. After all, they feel, we don't wait for a toddler to tell us in so many words if he's ready to be weaned, or ready to go to nursery school or ready to have a baby brother or sister.

If this way of thinking seems congenial to you, and if your child has the ability to use the potty, then there seems little harm in your taking the initiative. It seems obvious that many, many children have learned at their parents' request, and as long as the teaching is not harsh or premature, no harmful effects are observable. As long as you realize that you will have to keep "reading" your child after the diapers are off, and as long as you are flexible enough not to get into a battle of wills, you will probably do fine and so will your toddler.

If you do decide that you will be the one to initiate the switch from diapers to potty, take the following considerations into account:

Wait *at least* until the second birthday has passed (for a boy, you might wait until two and a half) before making the request, and don't associate the switch from diapers to pants directly with the birthday. After all, toilet learning, while an enormously satisfying accomplishment for a toddler, is nonetheless a responsibility, and one that's not so easy to master. The birthday should be a celebration with no strings attached; toilet learning should be a natural developmental step, associated with "being big enough now" or "being ready," rather than with being a certain age.

Before taking the step, you should also review your child's current life situation. Things should be as close to normal as possible. Ask yourself if there's been a recent change, such as the birth of a new baby, the loss of a regular babysitter, a change in playgroup or nursery school, or a death of a family pet. Don't switch to underpants right before or after you move to a new house, go on vacation or visit relatives for a week. A child might be under stress in such situations. Often small things that adults take in stride—such as a change in a parent's work schedule—can be stressful to a toddler.

Once you and/or your child have decided that he is ready,

the following step-by-step plan can serve as a guide to the first day out of diapers:

1. *Introduce the idea*: If your child hasn't requested it himself, you might say at breakfast one morning, "We think it is time for you (or "We think you are ready") to stop wearing diapers and start using the potty now." Make a positive statement; don't ask a question like "Do you want to stop wearing diapers?" unless you are willing to take no for an answer.

2. *Give advance notice*: Don't rush into things. Give your child time to get used to the idea. Set a date for later in the week to buy and start wearing the underpants. You might say, "On Thursday morning, we'll go shopping together for some big-boy pants." Choose a day when you'll be at home and when the atmosphere will be relaxed. Don't try to start your child in pants on a day when he's going to a birthday party or when you're expecting a crowd for lunch. If you are working parents, you may want to start on a Saturday. If not, a quiet weekday may be best.

3. *Give another reminder*: In a day or two, mention once again that the big day is coming up, but don't harp on it and don't build it up too much. A calm, matter-of-fact attitude will reassure your child.

4. *Call off the procedure if*: (1) your child responds with a vehement "NO!"; (2) your child is in a particularly negative mood or is out of sorts that week; (3) an unexpected event— such as the loss of an important person or an illness— disrupts everyday routines. Wait a few weeks until things are calmer and then begin again.

5. *When the big day comes*: Take your child with you to buy the underpants. Select several kinds that are acceptable to you, then let him choose the styles and colors he likes best from these. Be sure to buy them big enough so he'll be able to pull them up and down easily. And get enough: about a dozen pairs.

6. *At home, remove the diaper*: Help your child put on a pair of pants and store the others in a low drawer or on a shelf within his reach. Let him admire himself in the mirror and tell him he's a big boy. Explain that since he isn't wearing a diaper, he'll have to "put his pee-pee and BMs in the potty." Remind him to "tell mommy and daddy" when he has to use the potty.

7. *Lead him to the potty once*: Ask him to try to urinate if he can. If he does, praise him mildly, saying "Good" and smiling and giving him a little hug. Don't overpraise.

8. *Remind him once again*: "Remember, you're not wearing diapers now, so you'll have to use the potty."

9. *Now wait for accidents*: They are useful and necessary, because only from them will your child learn what is going on. At first, he may be amazed to see urine flowing from his new pants, because he doesn't really understand that they won't act like diapers.

10. *Be relaxed about accidents*: Don't panic—it's only a little water and can be easily mopped up. Express calm reassurance that "next time, you'll remember to tell mommy you have to pee in the potty." It isn't even necessary to say "*Try* to remember," which puts the pressure on to try. Your

reassurance that he *will* learn is all that is needed. Some children are upset about spoiling the pants and need to be assured that they'll be as good as new after being washed.

11. *After an accident*: Lead your child to the potty "to see if any more comes out." This exercise reminds him where the urine should have gone. Help him get and put on a new pair of pants.

12. *Don't flush away the contents of the potty*: Wait until your child has left the bathroom before flushing, especially for BMs. (See chapters 3 and 7 for more about some children's sensitive feelings about flushing.)

13. *At naptime and at night*: Because dryness when sleeping usually comes a bit later than waking control, put your child back in diapers at bedtime. Simply explain that little children still use a diaper for bed and say that he will put the underpants on again when he wakes up. (For more on night dryness and when to expect it, see chapter 6.)

14. *From now on*: For the next few days, observe how your child is managing this new skill. If he never makes it to the potty and seems bewildered about what is going on, assume you've made a mistake about readiness and postpone toilet teaching for another month or two. If he does well and the accident rate stays within bounds, keep him in pants for all waking activities.

(Note: Please do not use the above guidelines before following the advice in chapter 3 to prepare your child for toilet learning.)

# No More Daytime Diaper: Step by Step

*A word about underpants*: Should you buy training pants or regular underpants? Some parents prefer regular underpants. If a child is a big wetter, they reason, training pants won't stop the flood anyway, and they'll just take a longer time in the dryer. And if the pants are effective in absorbing the urine, they may be working against the learning process. Said one child-care worker, "What we want the child to learn is that he is not wearing a diaper, and that if he urinates, there will be consequences." Other parents, however, prefer training pants. They feel less anxious about accidents knowing that there is some protection between their toddler and their wall-to-wall carpet. And some parents keep training pants for outings, when a degree of absorption may be appreciated.

As described in the step-by-step guide, it's best to save the underpants for the day when the child makes a permanent switch from diapers. The potty has been around for a time and the child has been practicing on it. But the pants should be special. Then they will serve as what psychologists call a "discriminative stimulus"; that is, they will be a constant visual and tactile reminder that something is different, that the child now must use the potty. They are also a tangible sign that she has taken a step forward, that she is a big girl. As such, they are a kind of reward and a symbol of an important rite of passage.

Traditionally, parents haven't always made such a clean break from diapers, especially in times when toilet teaching was started a little too early. It was not uncommon for a mother to put her child in underpants for a few hours in the morning, then slowly extend the time until he was comfortable and reliable in pants at home. Once this was accomplished, underpants would be used on short outings and then longer ones, until eventually the child was wearing pants most of the time. If you are at home with your child every day, this approach may seem congenial to you.

In general, however, it will be confusing for a child to be switched back and forth between pants and diapers, and research has shown that parents whose children learned to use the toilet most easily made a clear switch to pants. It seems that the best route is to wait until the child is really ready before introducing underpants in the first place.

If you do decide to use the gradual method, be prepared to make it clear early on that diapers are no longer an everyday option. In her book *Your Baby & Child: From Birth to Age Five*, developmental psychologist Penelope Leach says, "Once he is more or less reliable at home in the daytime, abandon diapers as part of his regular clothes.... Although you will still get a fair number of pools, giving up diapers is important. While he still wears them sometimes, the child cannot finally learn that *every* feeling of bladder fullness means a trip to the potty. You cannot expect him to think 'I'm going to pee in a minute; am I wearing diapers or not?'"

It is well to remember that the switch to underpants is not the end but the beginning of the true learning period. Just as knowing how to roller skate is not the same as acquiring the ability to skate without falling, knowing how to use the potty must be followed by a practice period, during which the child masters a new skill. Remember that no child does this all at once. It takes a period of trial and error, one that may last for two weeks, two months, or even longer. Chapter 5, "The Learning Period," tells you what to expect and how to get through it gracefully.

# 5. The Learning Period

After his son had been in underpants for three weeks, a father was heard to say in an exasperated tone, "What I don't understand is how long this whole thing is supposed to take!"

Indeed, the learning period can be the most frustrating time for parents because it is hard to know what to expect. Some children are dry from the first day. ("She always was a camel," joked the mother of one of these lucky few.) But most children have difficulties acquiring the new skill of self-control, and for the first weeks and months after giving up diapers, the accident rate may be fairly high—one or two a day. On the average, children are not completely reliable until between ages four and five. Accidents will occur with decreasing frequency until they all but disappear by kindergarten. Until that happens, you'll want to help your child have as much success as possible.

*Provide easy clothing*: Dress the learner in easy-to-handle clothes—loosely fitting pull-on pants, shorts, dresses, or skirts. No overalls or zippered jeans for now, please. You don't want unnecessary delays in getting down underpants and you want your child to be learning how to handle his clothing himself.

For a while, keep on accompanying your toddler to the bathroom—it shouldn't be a place where she feels lonely. You should be there for support, encouragement, and actual physical help when she needs it. A suggestion from psychologists is that parents initially be there to help, then gradually "fade" as they are no longer needed, so that the child achieves independence by slow increments. An example of this sort of fading is in helping your child learn to pull down her pants. First you may do it for her. Next, you place your hands over hers and firmly guide them down with the pants. As you feel her pulling, you ease your pressure and gradually take your hands away. If you see her struggling, don't just do it for her—put your hands over hers again, guide them over the rough spot, then remove your hands. (This advice is given in the book *Toilet Training in Less Than a Day* by Nathan H. Azrin, Ph.D., and Richard M. Foxx, Ph.D., which is discussed briefly in chapter 7.)

*Give friendly reminders*: You'll want to help your child experience success on the potty by reminding her to go either at intervals of several hours or when you see that she needs to go. Psychologists have found that children whose parents remind them are more successful in learning than those whose parents do not. It's important, however, to keep the reminders relatively infrequent and to avoid turning them into frustrated nagging.

This advice, however, is easier said than done, because when a two-year-old is asked, "Do you have to go pee-pee?" he will almost invariably answer, "No." The parent knows in her heart that he really does have to go, but she can't get him to budge. Then when an accident occurs, she has to bite her tongue to keep from saying "I told you so." And the next time he says "no" to a reminder, she feels herself getting angry, and may get into an ineffectual argument with a child who just becomes more and more stubborn.

Here are a number of techniques recommended by parents to avoid such battles and to overcome a toddler's natural desire not to interrupt his play for a visit to the potty:

—*Suggest an experiment*: When your child is first in underpants, say at regular intervals of two or three hours, "It's time to go to the potty." If she says she doesn't have to go, don't argue with her. This may make her resist what she sees as a demand to produce. It's easier for her if you make it clear that you're not asking for instant results. Some parents suggest an experiment, "You don't have to go pee-pee. Just sit on the potty and see if anything comes out." Other parents say, "Let's have a little try."

—*Use your hands to help your voice*: Standing at the door of the room and calling is a sure way to fall into the habit of nagging, because when your child doesn't come, you have to repeat your reminder over and over again. The more you repeat, the harder it is to keep annoyance out of your voice. A more effective method is to go over to your child, put your hands on his shoulders and gently guide him to the bathroom while saying *once*, "It's time to go to the potty." This will get him into the habit of going when you ask him to. You should begin to "fade" your guiding hands as soon as he starts to comply with your request on his own. But do praise him occasionally for going right away when it's time.

—*Make the reminder part of another suggestion*: Presenting a trip to the potty as just one step in the process of doing something exciting can help. For instance, say, "First we're going to the potty and then we will make a peanut butter sandwich / get out all your blocks / call Grandma on the phone."

—*Give a choice*: Ask, "Would you like to use the big toilet or the little potty this time?" or, "Do you need help or can you manage alone?"

—*Offer to remind him beforehand*: Ask, "Would you like me to remind you or can you remember by yourself?" If you make the offer and he accepts, the eventual reminder doesn't seem like nagging because it was his decision.

—*Suggest using a timer*: Setting a timer makes the reminder seem like a game, and also puts you and your demands out of the immediate picture.

As time goes on, your child gets used to the routine of being reminded, and realizes what will happen if he doesn't interrupt himself to use the potty. Now you will want to "fade" the reminders, especially if he seems annoyed or insulted by them. The reminders of the first weeks of learning are for the child's benefit: they help her learn by increasing the chances of successful experiences and cutting down the number of failures. But constant reminders after the child has pretty much learned what is going on may actually slow down the process of mastery by placing the responsibility for remembering on the parent rather than on the child, where it belongs. Once accidents have become occasional, it is wisest to let the child assume responsibility for keeping dry.

## The Learning Period

*Children's feelings about accidents*: Most children are upset by toileting accidents. One child will cry piteously, while another will scream or whine to have his clothes changed. In either case, the child's unhappy feelings about the failure are sure evidence that she is motivated to outgrow accidents. Although there may be a temptation to scold the child and say, "See what happens when you don't go to the potty on time," this response is punitive and doesn't take advantage of the child's own desire to succeed. A more supportive response would be reassurance and a reminder to ask for help in the future.

There are children who do not show feelings about accidents and seem indifferent. In these cases, one may be tempted to scold the child in an effort to instill some sense of responsibility in him—to *make* him care. In fact, however, psychologists agree that this show of indifference probably means that he does care, perhaps a little too much, which is why he is afraid to show it. Again, reassurance that he will remember the next time and a reminder to "use the potty when you have to go" are in order. Over the long term, it may help to tell him that little children often have accidents but that you know he will outgrow them as he gets older.

*Your feelings about accidents*: Perhaps it is easy for you to cope with accidents. You feel relaxed, you know that the worst that can happen is a puddle to wipe up, and you have confidence that the rate of accidents will gradually diminish to almost zero by the end of the preschool period.

But not everyone is so sanguine. Some of us feel worried about going out with a toddler who may suddenly let loose a flood in public. We're afraid of being embarrassed or of inconveniencing others. And we tend to overidentify with the child, remembering times in our own childhood when we lost control and suffered embarrassment or ridicule as a result. So when our toddler shrieks, "I have to go pee-pee!" and runs for the bathroom holding her crotch, we feel the clutch of irrational panic: will she make it in time?! We wish she would outgrow accidents and relieve us of this kind of anxiety.

Other parents seem free of anxiety but feel annoyed with the child. They are ready and willing to be patient for a day or a week, but after a while, they feel "enough is enough." They are tired of changing wet clothes and want to be free of the child's dependency on them in this area. One father confessed, "Sometimes I would get angry at him and just say, 'When are all these accidents going to stop? We're trying to get you to urinate and make BMs in the toilet, and you keep on having all these accidents!'"

Sometimes parents are careful not to scold or shame the child when he is first starting, but once he has been at it for a while, they feel he ought to know better. Then it begins to seem appropriate to say things like "I'm so disappointed in you" or, "Aren't you ashamed of yourself, a big boy like you?" or, "You're not a baby anymore, you know!" In fact, however, these tactics are never appropriate, and shaming an older toddler may hurt him even more than a younger one, because he has more sense of his own identity and is more demanding of himself.

When parents are overly concerned, feel impatient, or act in a punitive way toward normal lapses in control, it may be because of underlying anxieties. On the surface, they may tell themselves that all is well, but deep down they may be afraid that the child's accidents mean they are not good parents. Good parents would have somehow taught their child more adequately, right? Or they may find it hard to trust that the child will eventually learn. What if he keeps on having these accidents in first grade? They may wonder if the accidents are directed against them. Maybe he's doing it for spite. Or they may feel that the lack of control shows that the child is basically lazy and needs discipline to avoid setting a precedent for slovenly habits in the future.

All of these ideas and feelings are common among parents, but none of them is objectively valid. Charles E. Schaefer, Ph.D., a child psychologist and the author of a book for professionals on children's toileting difficulties, says, "It is unlikely that children wet or soil because they are lazy, obstinate, or rebellious. Accidents are much more likely to be due to slow physiological development, insecurity-anxiety, or ignoring signals due to intense involvement in play." The appropriate responses to these three causes would be patience, reassurance, and gentle reminders, *not* punishment, shaming, or blaming. (For a further discussion of parents' feelings during toilet teaching, see chapter 8.)

*Regressions and other setbacks*: During the learning period, there will be times when the accident rate increases suddenly. The child seems to have forgotten everything he ever knew about using the toilet, and you may feel helpless and bewildered. It will help to remember that stress, tension, and changes in daily routines may all cause regressions in a toddler. Take stock of what has been happening in the child's life. The birth of a sibling, a separation from a parent, the death of a grandparent, the start of nursery school, even a cold or illness—any such occurrences could be the reason for a sudden setback in toilet learning. Usually all that is needed is to realize the cause, provide reassurance, and wait it out. Normally, these periods don't last much longer than a week.

Sometimes children can't cooperate with every aspect of toilet learning at once. It is not unusual for a child, especially a boy, to urinate consistently in the potty, but to withhold bowel movements. He may ignore his body's signal to defecate and become chronically constipated; he may simply make all his BMs in his pants; or he may start depositing his stools in a corner. If you have a child who is experiencing a regression; who is often constipated; who is withholding stools from the potty; or who seems to be teasing you with accidents, you are likely to be quite upset. Chapter 7, "Common Difficulties During Toilet Learning" will give you more information about understanding your child's behavior, handling your feelings, and helping the child through troubled periods.

*Deciding whether to postpone toilet teaching*: Suppose your child has just started in underpants and things don't seem to be going well at all. Perhaps she was cooperative and successful for the first day or two, but since then she's hardly used the potty. Should you call the whole thing off for a while?

In deciding whether or not to postpone toilet teaching, you'll want to determine if your child is simply undergoing a temporary setback, if your behavior is the cause of her troubles, or if you misjudged her readiness and started too soon.

You don't want to pop a toddler back into diapers at the first setback, for this will sabotage the process of toilet learning. For instance, if a child has been in underpants for a few weeks and is doing fine, then suddenly starts having a lot of accidents, you can assume he is having a normal period of regression, and you'll want to look for sources of stress, try to relieve pressure, and wait it out rather than rush back to diapers.

Sometimes a child will have a short setback at the very

start of learning, and you should give him a chance to recover before taking any action. The parents of a two-and-a-half-year-old described such a setback: "Peter had very few accidents during the first week he was in pants. All that week he was at his day-care center, and he kept getting better and better at getting to the potty on time. Then on Saturday, he kind of fell apart. We stayed home all day, and he had many, many accidents. We were beginning to wonder if perhaps he wasn't really ready. But on Sunday, the number of accidents fell dramatically—I think he had only three. These occasional accidents continued for about another week and then he stopped having accidents altogether."

Compare this experience with a child who does well the first day, then refuses to use the potty the next. For the first two weeks, the course of toilet learning is rocky and the family is tense. The child seems stressed, and although there are occasional "good" days, there are many more days when most of his urine and BMs end up either in his pants or on the floor—not in the potty. The parents *know* he is ready because they have experienced those good days. So they try to wait it out, and they may go through several months of conflict before either the child starts using the potty or the parents finally go back to diapers.

In a case like this, it seems safe to assume that the child is not emotionally ready, especially if he is closer to two than to three. Before making the decision to go back to diapers, the parents might examine their own feelings and behavior to see if they are overreacting to accidents; if they are communicating a sense of hesitancy to the child; or if they are putting too much pressure on him for perfection. And they might try to change their behavior accordingly. But if there is no improvement, and the child is not succeeding in using the potty fairly consistently after a week or two, it seems best to postpone toilet learning for a month or six weeks, and then start over.

The parents can say to the child, "It looks as if you don't feel like using the potty right now. Would you like to wear diapers again for a while?" They should make it clear that this is not a punishment for failing to perform on the potty, not a shameful defeat, but simply a postponement. And they should let him know that they have confidence in his ability to do well after he has had a little more time to grow.

*Gaining independence and developing good habits*: As he approaches and passes his third birthday, your child will probably be making progress in gaining independence and taking care of going to the toilet by himself. Some children become very grown up as time passes and may almost resent their parents' presence in the bathroom. "I want privacy," a child may intone, or, more imperiously, "Go out!" Most parents will welcome such an order and leave their child alone when he wants to be.

Boys at three will probably be standing to urinate all the time and their aim will be improving. They may still need a stool to help reach the big toilet.

Girls may go through a phase of wanting to stand up too, especially if they have observed boys using the toilet. A girl may even claim that she has a penis. There is no cause for alarm about this behavior, which is perfectly normal. The best way to handle it is to tell her matter-of-factly that she is a girl and does not have a penis; she has a vagina (or vulva), which is wonderful, and she will grow into a woman "like mommy" and be able to have babies. Letting her try to urinate standing up is the best way for her to find out that it doesn't work very well for her. Some girls discover their own version of standing up: sitting balanced on the toilet seat facing backward. They may go through a period of using this position, but eventually will come back to the usual, more comfortable way.

At first, most parents wipe toddlers, but after a while they expect the children to learn to do it for themselves. One parent told her child, "You'll be going to nursery school soon and you'll have to know how to wipe yourself." For others, it's a more gradual development: "I wiped him myself at first and then after a while he did it on his own."

Some children seem to want a parent's presence in the bathroom for a while longer and may use the wiping as a way of prolonging dependency. Even four-year-olds sometimes want their parents to wipe them. As one mother said, "She *can* wipe, but she won't." A way of moving away from this dependency as the child gets older is to teach her how to wipe and offer to come and "check" her. Then you can slowly "fade" the checking as she shows less need for the contact.

Pediatricians recommend that you teach your child to wipe thoroughly. If the job isn't quite done, don't finish it yourself, but encourage your child to do it (unless it is simply too messy for him to manage). Teach girls to wipe from front to back to avoid spreading fecal matter to the vaginal area and urethra, where it might cause urinary tract infection.

Developing the habit of handwashing is recommended too. Some parents insist on it after every use of the toilet, but others feel it is essential only after a bowel movement when the child did the wiping. When urination is frequent, as it is during the learning period, washing after every trip to the potty may become too much of a chore and may tempt the child to "forget" to use the potty. For the reluctant, you might try putting out pretty guest towels, fancy soaps, or liquid soap in a squirter bottle.

As they grow, children will learn to flush the toilet themselves, and having control over the flushing can help banish any leftover fears of the toilet. Waving bye-bye to the feces seems exciting to little children. Let your child remove the potty chamber and dump the contents in the toilet. You'll be surprised how careful three-year-olds can be. The mother of twin boys described her children learning to flush this way: "They were very proud to remove the pot, carry it to the toilet, and dump it. And they'd really look to see what was going in. They'd count the BMs and say 'how big' or 'how little.' It was very funny and cute. We'd flush and wave good-bye, and, oh, the fights they used to have about who was going to flush!"

*Great interest in "things of the toilet"*: A period of inordinate interest in stools is common during this time. A mother reported, "For a long time, he liked describing the different shapes. He would say things like, 'three pickle poops.'" Most parents take this behavior with a grain of salt and often find it amusing. But most of us would also be a little embarrassed by a child's public discussion in a loud, high-pitched voice of the size and consistency of a "horsie's poops" or by her excitedly pointing out a dog relieving itself by the curb. It can help to remember that the behavior only reflects the child's interest in something that is very important to her (and to you) right now, and her involvement in "the things of the toilet" is perfectly natural and, fortunately, temporary.

Sometimes this involvement may extend to a desire to touch the stools. Children may want to touch each other's productions in the potty, and some toddlers like to try stool-smearing. The parents' reaction to both events may be inward horror, but it's best not to respond with panic. Because a child at this stage is susceptible to anxiety about being dirty, and because you do not want to imply that the products of his own body may be "dangerous," it's not a good idea to emphasize dirt and germs. You don't want to shout, "That's filthy!" or, "That has germs! You'll get sick!" A matter-of-fact approach is better: "BMs are not for touching, they are for flushing" or "We don't touch BMs—just look."

The same approach is best when dealing with toddlers and preschoolers who go through a stage of indulging in "bathroom" jokes and bad language. A parental reaction of shock and disapproval is a surefire way to encourage this sort of thing. A child will do it just to see you react. With a young toddler, who is not yet aware of the social improprieties of this kind of talk, it's best to be bland and ignore it—it will go away. With an older child who uses the language to tease, you can remain bland, but say in a chiding way, "I don't like to hear that" or "That kind of talk isn't good manners." If the child continues and the situation seems to be getting out of hand, set limits on the behavior. You shouldn't act as if the child is "bad" because he uses bad words. Instead, emphasize consideration for others and separate him from the group until he is ready to behave better. You might say, "People don't like to hear those words, so you'll have to stay in your room until you are ready to speak in a more polite way." The punishment of isolation is appropriate to the offense of annoying others, and as soon as he demonstrates a willingness to behave better, he should be allowed to come out.

*Going out with a learner*: During the learning period, many parents find that outings are not what they used to be. One family always carried a couple of cloth diapers in a plastic bag (for mopping up unexpected puddles), and a father who had gone on many an urgent search for toilet facilities said, "You discover that there are bathrooms in places you never imagined." Some toddler homebodies become so attached to their own potties that they cry and scream when confronted with a strange toilet, so it's a good idea to introduce your child to unfamiliar bathrooms early. Most children are willing to balance on the big toilet, but if yours is uneasy, offer to hold her while she's on. Some parents like to carry a travel potty seat that folds to fit in purse or pocket, and you may prefer this if you are worried about unsanitary public toilets.

A long outing in the park or country where there are no bathrooms may be possible only if you're willing to let a young toddler urinate in the bushes. For boys, this presents no problem, but girls will need some help. Most can manage by squatting down, or by removing pants and shoes, spreading legs apart, and urinating on grass or sand (which prevents splashing).

To minimize the need for such measures, it's a good idea to insist on a visit to the potty before every outing. This is not as easy as it sounds. Most children will resist vehemently. If they don't feel a clear urge, they'll cry, "But I don't *have* to!" The parent may argue a bit, then give in. Inevitably, the child pipes up later in the supermarket line, "I have to go pee-pee." Every parent knows the feelings of frustration and righteous anger that well up at that moment! Most of us will yield to the temptation to blame the child, saying, "Why didn't you go at home when I told you to?" And to add to the frustration, he doesn't seem to learn his lesson. The next time, he'll be no more willing to go and will still insist, "I don't *have* to."

How to get past this problem? Just make a steadfast rule that no one leaves the house without having a try in the bathroom. Even follow the rule yourself. And if your child refuses, plump yourself down in a chair and say, "I'm not going until everyone has been to the potty." Using the earlier advice about overcoming resistance will help too. Never say, "You have to make pee-pee." Always say, "You don't have to go, you just have to try. Let's see if anything comes out."

As your young child matures, he will become more and more secure in his daytime toileting. Once he is doing consistently well during waking hours, and if you notice that he is often dry after a nap, you can try leaving him in underpants instead of putting him in a diaper at naptime. If he succeeds at staying dry, well and good. If not, use the diaper again until you notice more dry naps. Because the ability to stay dry at night usually comes well after daytime control and varies greatly from child to child, you can stop worrying about it for now. Chapter 6 will tell you how to cope while your child is still wet at night, and how to proceed when he is ready to stay dry.

# 6. Dry at Night: When?

There are children who simultaneously become dry at night and in the daytime. For most children, however, nighttime control takes longer than many parents realize. "I thought I knew about toilet teaching," one mother reminisced. *"What I thought I knew was that you didn't start daytime training until your child was waking up dry in the morning. It's a good thing a friend set me straight, because my son didn't stop wetting at night until he was four!"*

Children usually stay dry at night when daytime control has been consistently established and when their bladders are mature enough. A study showed that the majority of three-year-olds had stopped wetting at night, but nonetheless, night wetting is common until age five and not at all unheard of at six and seven, especially among boys.

*Wait for readiness*: Pediatricians and child-care experts unanimously advise that you continue using a diaper at night when your child is first learning to wear pants during the day. A child is definitely not ready for night dryness if: he is still accident-prone or urinates every couple of hours during the daytime; has a wet diaper by 9:00 P.M. when he is sleeping; or wets several times a night. So just relax for a while if this is the case with your child, and don't pressure him to stay dry, since this can actually impede the process of maturation by causing tension and anxiety.

Meanwhile, keep your eyes open for signs of readiness for nighttime control. These include some or all of the following: has few daytime accidents; is more or less upset about accidents; sometimes lasts for three or four hours in the daytime without urinating; often remains dry through naps; is occasionally dry in the morning; and sometimes wakes up early to urinate in the potty. As with daytime control, you can help by letting him know that you're confident he will outgrow the need for a night diaper as he gets older.

Occasionally, you can try leaving off the diaper if he shows some of the above signs, and often the child will ask to do without it on his own. A mother related, "About a month after he started being dry in the day, he told me he didn't want to wear a diaper at night. I wasn't sure he was ready, because all his friends were still wearing nighttime diapers, but I said, 'All right,' and we just started. I think he had two accidents and that was it."

If you try this and it doesn't work, go back to the diaper and try again later. Or you can leave it up to the child, as this family did: "He goes back and forth. If he says he doesn't want a diaper, then we usually don't use one. But if he says he does, then we usually put one on him." Read the child and be positive in your thinking, and the need for a night diaper will gradually diminish.

*Occasional wet beds*: Once children are consistently dry at night, you can still expect occasional nighttime accidents, perhaps as often as once every week or two. Some children will sleep through till morning after they have wet, but those who are heavy wetters will really soak everything—pajamas, sheets, even blankets and quilts. Then they get chilled and wake up crying in distress. Although it is fatiguing to get up in the wee hours to change a wet bed, resist expressing any annoyance. Just as we shouldn't scold a child who has an accident when learning daytime control, we shouldn't scold him for accidents when he's trying to master night control. A child doesn't wet the bed on purpose and is usually upset when an accident happens and may need some reassurance. However, try not to make changing the bed a social occasion. Just help clean up and go back to bed. You don't want to provide an incentive for getting you up at night.

Heavy wetters, of course, need help in the middle of the night. But children who just make a wet patch on the sheet may be taught to handle things themselves if they wake. One mother described how her son learned to do this: "We just told Patrick that everyone has accidents and sometimes he might wet the bed. We said, 'On this little chair are some spare pajama bottoms and a towel. If you have an accident, don't worry about it. You can just get up, change your pajamas, spread the towel over the wet spot and go back to sleep.'

"The first few times, he would come in to us crying. And we would go back with him and say, 'It's all right. You just had a little accident. We don't need to make a big fuss. Now here is everything, remember? That's right, take off the pajamas, put on the dry . . . now spread out the towel . . .' He needed a little help at first, but after about three times, he would just do it himself.

"I didn't think it was good to create a lot of hoopla about changing the bed at night. You know, everyone comes out and the lights go on as if wetting the bed is a big deal. We kept everything low key, as if nothing very important had happened. I would even wait until he wasn't around before changing the sheets the next day."

Those parents who don't get up with their children to clean up at night feel that this helps them get over the night wetting faster. Some tell the child to finish the night on a sofa or in a sleeping bag.

A way that may help prevent night accidents is to put the child's potty next to her bed. You can leave a night light on or paint the potty seat with luminous paint. The child is told before bed, "If you have to go in the night, get up and use the potty." Some parents insist that the child get up on her own; others feel this is asking too much of a little child and reason that if she is timid about getting up by herself, she may not use the potty, so they ask her to call if she needs company.

*Nighttime setbacks*: A child who has been dry at night for a while may experience a regression when she is sick, overly excited, under stress, or even just sleeping in a strange place. All that's needed in these situations is reassurance, a little extra love and patience. If the child is upset about the accidents, explain that little children sometimes have this trouble but they get over it in a short time. It may help to talk about the source of the stress during the day, if you can figure out what it is. For instance, a mother whose child was wetting the bed several times a night on vacation brought along photos of home the following year and they talked about how much the child missed her home and her friends.

You want to communicate your confidence that the setback will be only temporary, so it isn't advisable to put the child back in diapers at the very start of a regression. To contain the flood, you may try putting waterproof pants over training pants. Another tip for dealing with a run of wet beds is to "double sheet" the bed, that is, first put on a waterproof sheet and then a cloth sheet, and on top of these another waterproof sheet and another cloth sheet. Then when the bed is wet at 3:00 A.M., all you do is strip off the top two and *voilá* the bed is made and ready to go again.

Occasionally, a child has a nighttime regression that doesn't resolve itself in a few days or a week. Instead, the bed is wet every night for weeks or even months. In a case like this, being flexible about the diaper is the wisest course. Ask if he would like to have a nighttime diaper again for a while until this period of wetting passes. Having the reassurance of a diaper again might even help to ease whatever tension he's under and speed up the recovery time.

*Late bloomers*: A late bloomer is different from the child who *was* dry at night and is experiencing a regression, or the child who is usually dry and has an occasional regression. A late bloomer may be dry during the day, but he doesn't become dry at night and continues to wet the bed after age three—either every night or several nights a week. Although parents sometimes become concerned about lateness, there is no reason to assume that a chronic problem will develop. As with daytime control, children develop at different rates for night dryness. Studies have shown that 20 to 25 percent of four- and five-year-olds still wet the bed, but the percentages decline dramatically with increasing age. If you are worried, you may want to discuss the matter with your child's doctor, who can examine her to rule out possible physical causes. (For information on bed-wetting in children over five, see chapter 7.)

Sometimes parents, confronted night after night with a wet bed, become angry at the child. Said one mother, "Alison was a big four-year-old. She was wearing size six clothes and the 'toddler' size diapers didn't fit anymore. And she would wet the bed several times a week. When she did, I would be really angry at her because I suspected that she was doing it on purpose, either out of some hidden spiteful feelings or just to get attention in the middle of the night. Sometimes I would even yell at her, and then she would cry and cry." Another parent confessed that he thought there must be something wrong with his four-and-a-half-year-old son: "I thought we had messed him up somehow psychologically. I had visions of him ending up on the psychiatrist's couch because of something we had done."

Experts agree, however, that children do not wet the bed on purpose and that, especially under the age of six, bed-wetting is probably due to slow maturation or stress, rather than to spite or deep-seated emotional problems. In his book on toileting problems in children, Dr. Charles E. Schaefer says, "The ideas that the child [wets the bed] out of spite/hostility or a way to gain attention are almost unanimously rejected by professionals. . . . There is just no evidence to support these positions." And it is clear that negative reactions like ridiculing or punishing a child for wetting the bed won't help and can make matters worse.

*Practical tips and suggestions*: While patience is the best policy with late bloomers, the following ideas from child-care specialists and parents who've "been there" can make life easier for you and possibly encourage the child to out-grow the night wetting habit:

—*Double sheet the bed*: As suggested earlier, put on two sets of sheets: a waterproof sheet and a cloth sheet, and then another waterproof sheet and another cloth sheet. To change the bed, just pull off the top two.

—*Pad the child well*: Keep a younger child in diapers if he has *no* success with night dryness. If he gets too big for disposable diapers, you can use a cloth diaper, or try training pants with waterproof pants over them.

—*Change to pants when the child starts having some success*: Keep watching for signs of readiness and a desire to be dry at night. Then switch to pants to communicate that you believe nighttime control is now possible.

—*Have the child urinate just before sleep*: Make a trip to the potty be the *very* last thing the child does before going to bed. If there's a delay between potty and bed—for instance, if the child successfully begs for another story—make sure he has another try at urinating.

—*Keep the child warm*: There is some evidence that being chilled can diminish the amount of urine the bladder can hold. So make sure the child is warm enough in bed. If necessary, have the child wear a blanket sleeper.

—*Put the potty near the bed*: As already suggested, putting the potty right next to the bed with a nightlight on, or with the potty seat painted with luminous paint, may help if the child can wake up to use it.

—*Suggest waking up to use the potty*: Occasionally, mention that the potty is beside his bed if he needs to urinate in the night. Offer to get up and keep him company if he calls. If he resists, however, don't pressure him. The parent's attitude should be one of friendly helpfulness.

—*Teach the child to clean up himself*: Follow the advice

of the mother quoted earlier and show the child how to change his own pajamas and spread a towel over the wet spot. Suggest that he can handle things himself and doesn't need to wake you.

—*Encourage using the potty upon waking in the morning*: If you suspect that the child is making it through the night but urinating in bed as he wakes up, suggest trying to hold it until he can get to the potty. Offer to come and help if he calls.

—*Praise him for dry nights*: Experts say that children whose parents praise them when they do not wet the bed (and don't comment when they do) have more success in overcoming night wetting. Some behavioral psychologists suggest making a gold star chart for dry nights if the child is interested.

—*Be positive and encouraging*: Rather than dwell on accidents, emphasize the successes and suggest to the child that as time goes on, he will have more and more of them. One mother said, "I tried to create in my son the idea that he was gaining control of staying dry at night and the expectation that he would succeed."

The following practices, which many parents of late bloomers recommend, are controversial and often discouraged by professional child therapists:

—*Toileting the child at 10:00 or 11:00 P.M.*: The practice of putting the child on the toilet at the parents' bedtime is the measure people seem to rely on most in coping with continuing night wetting. The idea is either to wake the child and have her walk to the toilet or to carry the sleeping child to the bathroom. Some children will wake, while others will go through the whole process, even stumbling to the bathroom, in a state of sleep.

With a very young child who may be wetting several times a night, toileting him at the parents' bedtime may not help at all. Then a while later, when he has grown up a bit, it may start working. Some children will resist toileting that interrupts sleep and it's best not to get into a conflict with a child over this.

One mother described her experience with toileting her daughter at night: "Janet wasn't dry at night at three years old and I was beginning to think it was a big problem, when my sister-in-law said, 'Don't worry. Timmy wasn't dry until he was seven. We just took him to the bathroom at eleven P.M. He would urinate and go back to bed and never even wake up.' So I tried it with Janet. I would carry her to the bathroom before I went to bed and lo and behold it really helped to keep the bed dry. Her accidents went down to once or twice a week, instead of almost every night. What a relief!

"And when she got too heavy for me to carry, I put the potty next to the bed and sort of guided her onto it. When she was about four and a half, I started experimenting—every once in a while I would skip putting her on the potty. At first, she always wet the bed when I did this, but after a while she would occasionally stay dry. Then there was the wonderful night when she got up by herself to go to the bathroom at midnight. She did this for a while, then started sleeping through the night altogether at about five years."

Despite the fact that many parents like Janet's mother swear by this method and claim that it "saved their lives," research has shown that toileting the child late at night does not "train" the child to outgrow night wetting: if the parents stop toileting, the bedwetting will continue exactly as before. And many experts believe that toileting bed-wetters may actually prolong the habit, especially if children don't wake up, because it teaches them to urinate while they are asleep, which is exactly what is *not* wanted. Therefore, if parents want to practice night toileting, it is recommended that they make sure the child wakes up completely and walks by himself to the toilet.

—*Withholding evening liquids*: Many parents of late bloomers make a rule against drinking liquids after 7:00 P.M., but it is not clear even to the parents themselves whether the practice has any real effect on wetting. It certainly can create bitter conflicts between parents and a thirsty child, and psychologists say that withholding liquids can actually result in more bed-wetting. One expert feels that a child who goes to bed thirsty is more likely to wet because water will be on his mind, and a study has shown that withholding fluids may induce irritation of the bladder neck and cause frequent urination when the bladder is only partly full.

Some parents feel it is wise to avoid the bedtime juice bottle and carbonated beverages, but a cup of water to quench thirst will do no harm.

*Don't worry under age five*: Doctors advise parents not to worry about bed-wetting in children five and under. Only a small percentage of children between six and ten continue to wet the bed, and chances are that your child won't be one of them. So don't borrow trouble. Continue to follow the guidelines in this chapter for being patient and understanding, watching for signs of readiness for night dryness and encouraging the child to grow out of nighttime wetting.

# 7. Common Difficulties During Toilet Learning

Progress in toilet learning is often uneven, and parents learn quickly to expect occasional lapses. But sometimes problems arise that are puzzling and upsetting to even the most relaxed among us. Regressions, resistances, fears, bed-wetting, soiling—all are easy to handle in retrospect, but while they are happening, it's a rare parent who doesn't feel worried and confused. Knowing that other children and parents have gone through the same experiences and learning how they handled them can be a real help.

*Periods of regression*: In addition to the occasional accident, most children are susceptible to periods of regression due to stress. Usually these periods take parents completely by surprise. Everything is going along smoothly. Your child has been having spectacular success with toileting and has now started nursery school where she is doing nicely. You feel terrific—it seems as if your little girl has finally graduated from babyhood and smooth sailing is ahead. Then suddenly she starts having accidents all the time. No sooner is one cleaned up and reassurances given than another set of clothing is soaked. In this situation, parents feel frustrated, disappointed, and often completely bewildered.

To the old hand at raising toddlers, however, three words will stand out in the above description: *started nursery school*. And in other homes there are similar descriptions with other key phrases: he had a bad cold; she was excited about seeing her grandma; we spent a weekend in the country; friends were staying with us that week; his daddy went in for minor surgery; she didn't seem to be jealous of the new baby; his mommy was taking a new job.

To a young child, any change—for better or worse—can be stressful. And stress can bring on a regression—not only in toilet learning but in other skills such as dressing himself. Even changes within himself can cause stress. Often a child who has taken a major developmental step will suddenly regress. Parents wonder how a child who had seemed so grown up could turn so babyish again: sucking his thumb with a vengeance, cuddling his blanket, talking baby talk, and wetting his pants. It's as if he scared himself by moving forward too quickly and needs some time in retreat before going on again.

Most toileting regressions—that is, periods of wetting or soiling that follow periods of consistent control—are caused by stress, and the best way to deal with them is to be patient and understanding and to reassure the child both about the source of stress, if you think you know what it is, and about the wetting, which will pass. Scolding or pressuring the child to be more careful will usually have the opposite effect, because it will only make the child more nervous.

During periods of regression, you may wonder whether you should go back to diapers. There is no hard-and-fast rule about this and you'll have to play it by ear. Some people feel that it doesn't hurt to use diapers temporarily and it is certainly more convenient. Others believe that switching back and forth from pants to diapers is confusing to the child and makes her wonder if her parents are serious in their expectation that she will learn. You will have to decide which course to take based on your understanding of your child and your own tolerance for accidents. Do keep in mind that periods of regression are usually short and you may not really need to go back to diapers. In cases of diarrhea or prolonged regressions, you might try the half measure of putting waterproof pants over training pants instead of using a diaper. This arrangement keeps messes contained, but the child can still pull the pants down himself and go on the potty.

*Toilet learning, terrific—child, terrible*: Often toilet learning is going exceptionally well for a child. She learns rapidly and is very conscientious about staying dry. At the same time, however, other behaviors crop up that make living with her almost impossible. She may be cranky or fearful, have temper tantrums, get up often during the night, become annoyingly fussy about cleanliness, start dawdling a lot, or put up a terrible struggle about eating, bathing, or dressing. These difficulties may be stemming from the enormous amount of pressure she feels about being successful on the toilet. She may be waking because she is worrying about staying dry; she may be resisting her parents' requests for cooperation because she is being *too* cooperative about the toilet; and she may be driving everyone crazy about tiny specks of dust because she is driving herself crazy about keeping her pants clean. If her tensions are the result of too much pressure about toilet learning, it may help if the parents ease up on their requests and reassure her that perfection is not required.

*How to ease pressure*: Whether a child's stress is coming from outside demands or her own expectations, and whether it is expressed through renewed wetting or other tension outlets, you can help her cope by easing the general pressure in her life. There are a number of ways to do this:

—*Acknowledge the source of stress*: Letting the child know that you understand what is bothering her and sympathizing with her feelings are helpful. You don't necessarily have to change things and you won't want to talk her out of her feelings. Just acknowledge them with a few words. For example: "It's hard when mommy goes to work now and you can't see her as much as you want to."

—*Let her play baby*: Most children go through periods when they want to pretend to be a baby, and it can help them adjust to the new role of child. You won't want to initiate such games yourself, but if your child wants to cuddle on your lap and pretend to be your baby, go along with it. After the game is over, you can mention that you love her just the way she is and just as much as you did when she was little.

If she wants to talk baby talk, give her some leeway, even if it annoys you. You can set limits, such as no baby talk on the bus, but let her know that it's okay to pretend for a while.

—*Ease demands for good behavior*: If your child is going

through a period of stress related to toilet learning, don't pick this time to be extra demanding about other new grown-up behaviors. Diminish your expectations about table manners, independent washing, and dressing, even new social relationships. And don't keep commenting about how big he is getting. Keep in mind that all children have normal ambivalence about growing up and when they're feeling pressured, the wish to stay little comes to the fore. When they're feeling less put upon, they'll regain their enthusiasm for being big.

—*Show him that perfection is not required*: For the child who is feeling pressure about toilet learning, perfection may be his unconscious goal. He may somehow have gotten the idea that he is supposed to do this "just right." It will help not only to tell him outright that no one is perfect and that you don't expect him to be either, but also to demonstrate that you yourself don't have that goal in life. "The cake I made is crooked, but it will taste good anyway, won't it?" you might remark. Or, "I tore this envelope by accident, but I can just tape it. It's fine that way."

*Common fears related to the toilet*: A common difficulty in toilet learning is resistance to using the potty or toilet. Because there are a number of childhood fears related to the toilet, it's a good idea to watch for them if your child shows a resistance.

As was mentioned in chapter 3, a young toddler may fear that her feces, which she sees as a precious part of herself, will be flushed away. In addition to resisting the loss, she may be frightened that she herself could also be "swallowed up" by the toilet. This is because toddlers do not have an adult's concept of relative sizes. They simply do not know that they are too big to fit into such a small opening. Indeed, it is in an attempt to find out what fits into what that children of this age spend so much time putting objects into containers.

Another scary thing about the toilet is the noise it makes. Parents know that little children are often frightened of the vacuum cleaner because of its noise, but sometimes fear of the toilet's noisy flushing is less obvious. One mother had always known her child was leery of the toilet but didn't know why until one day the child said, "I'm always a little scared of the flushing because it makes a monster's roar." Sometimes the combination of the noise and the "swallowing up" makes children imagine that there's a monster in the toilet. In her classic book on early childhood, *The Magic Years*, psycholoanalyst Selma Fraiberg tells of a child who comes to her for treatment because of his refusal to use the toilet. Eventually he reveals his fear of the "lobster (monster) in the toilet," and after talking about it with Dr. Fraiberg for a while, he begins to use the toilet for the first time in his life.

Most children outgrow their fears without psychoanalysis, but there are several things parents can do to help them overcome concerns about the toilet:

—*At first, don't flush in a young toddler's presence*: If your young toddler seems disturbed by the toilet, avoid scaring him. Wait until he's left the bathroom before flushing away the contents of his potty.

—*Let the child play with the toilet*: If she likes to, let your child practice flushing before toilet learning becomes an issue. Perhaps showing her how it works inside the tank will help.

—*Tell him he's too big to be flushed*: Discuss relative sizes with your child and assure him that big objects can't fit into small holes. Demonstrate this with a number of objects and containers.

## Common Difficulties During Toilet Learning

—*Explain the sewer system*: Talking about how the "BMs go into a big pipe under the house and to a treatment plant" or "a septic tank" can help clear up any misunderstandings about the toilet as a devouring monster.

—*Wave bye-bye*: The ceremony of waving good-bye to the BMs seems to work because it acknowledges their importance to the toddler and helps him give them up more easily.

—*Let the child do his own flushing*: As soon as he is ready, let him flush the toilet himself. Having control over the flushing may make it less scary.

A less magical reason for being afraid of using the toilet or potty may be an association with a painful experience or shock. For instance, a toddler who lost her balance and slipped down into the toilet might avoid using it for a long time after, as might a little boy who hurt himself on a potty deflector. And a child who experienced pain on the potty while having a hard, constipated bowel movement might well conclude that it is safer to have BMs anywhere else but the potty. In cases like these, parents might not even remember the original trauma, but if they can trace the resistance to its source, they can usually help by reassuring the child that they will take away the danger, perhaps by holding the child on the toilet and teaching her to hold on to the seat herself, by removing the deflector, or by asking the child's doctor to prescribe a stool softener for painfully hard BMs.

If you suspect that your child is afraid of something but you can't find out what it is, your pediatrician may be able to help. Often a child will confide in someone other than the parents, who may be too close for comfort.

*Withholding BMs from the potty*: When they are first learning, some children find it hard to cooperate completely in the business of toileting. They may urinate consistently in the potty, but refuse to have their BMs there. Some hold back their BMs and become constipated; others may simply defecate every time in their pants; and others may even deposit their stools in corners or closets. Although a reluctance to have BMs in the potty is not uncommon, especially among boys, many parents don't know this, and if it happens to them, they wonder if something isn't terribly wrong. It seems as if the child is acting out of defiance, but actually it's just difficult for him to give in to all of his parents' demands at once.

The situation can be complicated because a child who withholds stools for long periods may become chronically constipated when feces become impacted in the rectum. Then moving the bowels will be painful and the pain will lead to more withholding and more constipation. The whole situation can become very distressing, so it's best to deal with it right away.

Dr. T. Berry Brazelton writes sensitively and knowledgeably about the problem in his book *Doctor and Child*. He recommends consulting the child's doctor at once. Rather than use enemas or suppositories, which can be painful and/or intrusive to the child, the doctor can prescribe stool softeners and a natural or mild laxative to prevent feces from becoming impacted. Then, advises Dr. Brazelton, parents should take any pressure to have BMs off the child. "If he or she is caught up in a struggle about where to have a BM," writes Dr. Brazelton, "say that the diaper is especially for this. Reassure the child that it is not important where the bowel movement takes place. . . . Offer a quiet place to hide or lie down, and assure the child that it is *his* or *her* choice, not yours. I would also be sure that you avoid other sources of pressure for a while—siblings who tease, peers or teachers who expect success, grandparents who shame. This is a time for reassurance and the comfort of being understood and protected."

In their book *Your Three-Year-Old*, Louise Bates Ames and Frances L. Ilg report that some parents have used an unusual method to help children who retain stools or leave them in inappropriate places. The parent spreads a newspaper on the bathroom floor and tells the child it's okay to have bowel movements there instead of the potty. This arrangement can make things easier for a child who has some fear or reluctance related to the potty, and it can help a toddler who simply finds it difficult at first to have a BM while seated. After a short time in the "puppy dog phase," the child can usually make a gradual transition from papers to the nearby potty.

Withholding stools from the potty is a most disturbing behavior and parents often resort at one time or another to scoldings and punishments—none of which has any effect whatsoever on the behavior, as any parent who has gone through it can attest. Parents should try to get help from the child's doctor and give the child time to get over it. If the problem isn't resolved in a few months, they should seek help from a child psychologist. (For a discussion about finding a psychologist, see the last section of this chapter.)

*Deliberate, naughty "accidents"*: So far, the problems discussed have all been unconscious difficulties due to slow maturation, outside pressures, or emotional conflicts within the child. In many cases, parents misinterpret these setbacks as signs of defiance, stubbornness, or misbehavior and try to correct them through discipline. When the trouble is not a discipline problem, however, it is very easy to find that out: discipline has no effect whatsoever on it. Instead, understanding, love, and giving the child room to grow are the answers to developmental and emotional needs.

Occasionally, however, a child discovers that he can use "accidents" to tease his parents or to "punish" them when he is angry. One mother recalled, "She stood there and said, 'If you don't let me have another cookie, I'm going to pee on the floor.' And when I didn't give her the cookie, she actually went ahead and did it!"

Another parent said, "I would be on the phone and he would want my attention, and I'd be saying 'Just a minute, just a minute, I'm on the phone.' And then he would wet his pants."

Other parents reported that children deliberately wet or soiled themselves when the parents were busy taking care of a new baby or when their attention was taken up by a visitor.

In dealing with behavior like this, you should try to be very sure that the accident was in fact a deliberate attempt to get your attention or to punish you. If the child has only recently started staying dry, perhaps it was a genuine accident that coincided with other events to make it look purposeful. If you think this is what happened, then treat it like any other accident.

If the child has considerable control, however, and you are quite sure the "accident" was deliberate, then your course of action should be in two parts. The first part is in handling the immediate "accident" in a way that will discourage its repetition. The second part is to respond to the child's indirect plea for more attention. These two parts are best kept separate.

In dealing with the deliberate "accident," you want to act in such a way as to make it unlikely that the child will get into the habit of using this method of getting his way or of gaining attention. Therefore, you do not want to let him get what he wants *as a direct result* of deliberate soiling or wetting. What he wants is your immediate reaction, and even parental anger or punishment is gratifying to a child who is feeling ignored. Therefore, your response should be as unemotional and matter-of-fact as possible. The child is trying to provoke you, and your getting upset, showing anger, or being cold and icy all play into this game. The idea is to *act* matter-of-fact, while *saying* that this behavior makes you angry and is definitely not acceptable to you. One father recalled that he remained placid and told his child very firmly, "We like playing baby games with you, but we don't like playing these baby games. When you play these baby games it just makes us angry." Then he pointed to the child's potty and said, "The house is not a potty. This is the potty."

Another way of not gratifying the child's desire for immediate attention is not to clean him up in a big hurry. Of course, you wouldn't want to leave him crying for a long time and you wouldn't want to egg him on to further destructive acts by seeming to ignore him even more. But you don't want to give the impression that he can make you jump like a puppet on a string by soiling himself. You could say, "I want to put some water on to boil in the kitchen. You come along and then I'll help you get cleaned up." If he is crying and carrying on, let him, but keep your own attitude matter-of-fact.

You can also help discourage the behavior by emphasizing that you are only helping the child clean himself up. Depending on his age and manual dexterity, you may in fact have to do a good portion of the messy work, but he can mop up a puddle, finish wiping or washing himself, and help rinse out the soiled pants. Then emphasize that he wash his hands thoroughly—make him do it again if the job isn't quite done—and finally have him put on clean clothes. All this should be done without a punitive air, but rather in a no-nonsense way, as if to say, "This is what you have to do if you make a mess." A parent shouldn't be fun or interesting to be with while the cleaning up is taking place. Limit your remarks to the instructions about the task at hand and don't react to other things. Your attitude should be, "Later we can talk, later we can play, later we can do lots of interesting things. But now we have to clean up."

This approach, of course, needs to be tempered according to the child's age. A child who is almost four and who wets to get her own way can be expected to clean everything herself. A child who is almost three and who is jealous of a new baby should not be expected to complete a long series of cleaning-up tasks.

The businesslike attitude that emphasizes cleaning up is much more effective for deliberate "accidents" than meting out a punishment, such as sending the child to his room or withholding a favorite toy or activity. Punishment keeps the issue alive and increases parental involvement, which was what the child wanted from the behavior in the first place. The down-to-earth expectation that he must clean up when he purposely makes a mess shows clearly that there are real consequences to his action and that he, and not the parent, is responsible.

While you shouldn't gratify the child's desire for attention and love at the time of the "accident," you'll certainly want to think about things and see if he is feeling a bit neglected. He may be reacting to a realistic situation in which you've been extra busy, or he may be feeling lonely because he thinks a new baby has replaced him in your affections. In either case, you'll want to give him some extra love and attention, which doesn't necessarily mean giving him more *time* than you normally would.

Wait until the impact of the "accident" has receded, then offer to spend some special time with the child. He may need to be *told* that you love him, that you enjoy being with him, and that you want to spend time paying attention to him. Telling him these things may mean more than just doing them. If the child has been pestering you a lot for attention, it can help to seek him out at a moment when he isn't asking for contact. You don't want to keep interrupting him when he is interested in something else, but let him know that you don't just forget about him when he isn't reminding you he's there.

When you are very busy—say with work or with an infant—it can help to plan one special time of day to be with the child alone. Talk about that special time during the times when you can't give him your full attention: "I can't do that with you now because I have to feed the baby, but later we'll have our own time. I really look forward to our being together, don't you?"

By using this two-part approach in handling purposeful soiling and wetting, you may be able to put an end to the behavior after only one or two incidents. However, if it keeps on happening, do get some professional help, as this is one form of self-expression that should not be allowed to become a habit.

*Bed-wetting and other problems in older children*: There is no need to worry about bed-wetting in children of five and under. Many children, especially boys, take that long to stay dry at night, because during sleep there is less conscious control of the body. (The fact that little children often fall out of bed is evidence enough of that.) If you are concerned about night wetting in younger children, please reread chapter 6, "Dry at Night: When?"

If you have followed the guidelines in chapter 6 and if your child is still one of the small percentage of children who continue to wet the bed after age five, you will probably want to do something about it. Paying no attention to the problem in older children or waiting for them to outgrow it is unfair to them. They may be teased by other children, will not be able to sleep away from home, and will most likely develop some negative feelings about themselves. Helping your child gain control of his night wetting will improve his self-esteem.

In past times, it was not uncommon to try to "cure" bed-wetters with various punitive methods that often bordered on child abuse. Such methods, however, are not only cruel, they are completely ineffective. They make no change in the wetting, but only succeed in making the child feel resentful, guilty, and ashamed of himself for behavior over which he has no conscious control.

The first step in helping a child with bed-wetting is to elicit his cooperation in overcoming the problem. Even if he adopts an I-don't-care attitude, this is probably a defense, and he most likely wants very badly to stop wetting the bed. If your attitude is that of a friendly helper, the child will probably be grateful for the chance to do something constructive about his bed-wetting.

First you will want to discuss the situation with the child's doctor. If there are no physical causes for the problem, you might want to read more about it. Two excellent books to consult are *Childhood Encopresis and Enuresis: Causes and Therapy* by Charles E. Schaefer, Ph.D., which is a fairly technical and comprehensive book on children's toileting problems, and *How to Help Children with Common Problems* by Charles E. Schaefer, Ph.D., and Howard L. Millman, Ph.D., which has an excellent chapter on bed-wetting. Both books give information about the problem and practical advice for parents.

You may be tempted to purchase a mechanical device, usually called the "bell and pad," which wakes the child as she is wetting, and thus trains her over a period of weeks or months to wake before wetting, and eventually to hold the urine and keep on sleeping. The book *A Parent's Guide to Bedwetting Control* by Nathan H. Azrin, Ph.D., and Victoria A. Besalel, Ph.D., presents a program to follow using this apparatus, and you might want to try it as a last resort. In general, however, the bell and pad is best used with the supervision of a therapist. Studies have shown that parents using the device on their own have a lower rate of success than those using it with professional guidance.

Another reason for finding a good therapist is that he or she will be able to evaluate the needs of your particular family and decide on the treatment that is best for you, one which may not necessarily involve the bell and pad method.

It may reassure parents to know that bed-wetting is not usually a sign of deep emotional disturbance in children. Research has shown that four out of five older children who wet the bed are normal and well adjusted. It is also comforting for a child to be told that bed-wetting is a common childhood problem and that he is not alone in having this difficulty.

Today, when there are a number of effective treatments used by therapists that usually eliminate the problem in a matter of months, there is no reason for a youngster to go through the childhood years labeled a bed-wetter and suffering the shame and self-doubt associated with the problem. So if you are unsuccessful in coping with the difficulty yourself, do seek professional help.

—*Lack of daytime bladder control*: A very small number

of children—girls more often than boys—continue to have frequent daytime accidents after the preschool years. In some cases, this is caused by forgetfulness and overinvolvement in play, and the solution is more frequent reminders and praise for remembering to get to the bathroom in time.

In other cases, the problem is associated with urinary infections which cause uncontrollable urination. Naturally, the first step will be to consult the child's doctor so the urine can be examined for possible infection. However, clearing up an infection is often not the solution to the difficulty; many times the accidents continue even after the infection is gone. In these cases, the lack of control may be stress related.

Usually a child will outgrow the problem with age, but a course of treatment with a child psychologist might help a nervous child learn to deal with stress sooner.

—*Soiling in older children*: As discussed earlier in this chapter, a child's refusal to have bowel movements in the potty when he is first learning is not uncommon and should be treated with loving patience. If the child continues soiling after the age of three, however, or begins to do it for the first time later in childhood, you will definitely want to do something about it. Parents report that they have had success with the following tactics: the child was given a reward for every bowel movement deposited in the potty or toilet; the child was expected to clean up after soiling; the child was not allowed to wear dresses to nursery school (something she liked to do) until she had stopped soiling for two weeks, and a favorite caregiver in the child's day-care center stopped cleaning him up and was replaced in this chore by a caregiver he didn't like as well. If these or similar tactics don't work for you, you will definitely want to seek professional help without delay. Again, this behavior does not usually mean that a child has psychological problems, but it should not be ignored, as it will have serious social consequences for the child.

—*Very late bloomers*: Some experts say that parents need not worry about slow developers until after three and a half or four, but it is a rare parent who will not be concerned about a child who has not started using the potty at all for either urine or BMs soon after the third birthday. If you are disturbed by slow learning or by a long-term resistance, you will want to discuss the situation with your child's doctor to rule out physical causes. Between you, you may be able to determine if there is some emotional reason for the delay. Your doctor may advise you that your child is simply later than other children, or he or she may be able to give you some suggestions based on experience with hundreds of other toddlers.

If it seems that for some reason your child simply doesn't know what to do, you can start all over again, as if she were eighteen months old. Reread chapters 2 and 3 in this book and begin again. Observe her for signs of readiness, and prepare her for toilet learning by teaching her about her body and about the toilet. You'll also want to make very sure that you communicate clearly that you fully expect her to learn to use the toilet like other children and adults she knows. After the preparation period, you will want to follow the advice in chapter 4 for no more daytime diaper.

If your child seems to have a particularly hard time with this, you might want to follow the program in the book *Toilet Training in Less Than a Day* by Nathan H. Azrin, Ph.D., and Richard M. Foxx, Ph.D. While the title suggests that the emphasis is on the rapidity of the learning, the program was first devised not for speed, but to help the retarded learn a complicated skill. Because the method maximizes learning, researchers found that when it was used with children of normal intelligence, they learned amazingly fast.

For most children, I would not recommend *Less Than a Day* because it seems overly manipulative, using frequent rewards of sweet drinks and snack foods, and because it involves the use of what psychologists call "overcorrection" or punitive consequences for accidents. For instance, toddlers routinely have to clean up after accidents and have to "practice" moving quickly to the potty from various points in the house *ten times* after each accident. Although the authors claim that children are "trained" and happy after only a day or two of this intensive program, other researchers have found that many parents fail with it because the procedure is complicated, and that many children have temper tantrums and avoid the potty in response to the overcorrection. It seems much better for most toddlers to learn gradually and for parents to praise success and be understanding about accidents.

However, if other methods have failed for you and your four-year-old, you may want to discuss the matter with your pediatrician and try this book. An older child might well cooperate with the technique and be interested in trying it out.

You might want to take a different approach if your four-year-old seems to understand everything about toileting and elimination and has considerable control but for some reason refuses to use the potty. Confronted with this problem, several parents have succeeded in getting past the block by offering rewards. In general, I would not recommend rewards because I feel they tend to preempt the child's satisfaction with his own growth and autonomy. However, in some cases they have helped parents and children out of a difficult resistance.

## Common Difficulties During Toilet Learning

One child, for instance, had considerable control. She refused to use the potty and toilet, but neither would she wet or soil in pants or on the floor. She would remain dry for many hours and then insist on having a diaper put on when she needed to go. Her mother had tried everything and had just about given up. Then one day she decided to sit with the little girl in the bathroom for as long as it took, while promising an ice-cream cone as a reward for going in the potty. "At first she would cry and cry for a diaper and it took forty-five minutes for her finally to go," said the mother. "But once she realized that there really would be an ice-cream cone at the end of it, the time went down to fifteen minutes. In about a week, she was going to the bathroom all by herself and I discontinued the rewards."

Another parent reported her experience in the August 1981 issue of *Redbook* magazine. She had been loath to put any pressure at all on her son, believing that a totally accepting atmosphere would foster learning. The boy, however, did not finally learn until his mother sought the advice of a psychologist. On the therapist's recommendation, she wrapped a lot of party favors and little toys in colored papers and placed them in a glass bowl on the top of the refrigerator. Then she simply told the child that he would be allowed to pick a surprise package every time he had a BM in the potty. From that moment on, he had *every* bowel movement in the potty.

It seems that in both these cases, the children and their parents had gotten "stuck" in a fixed way of seeing themselves and each other and couldn't get unstuck without somehow losing face. The external rewards worked because through them the parent told the child, "I really mean it this time," and they were attractive enough to let the child leave his stubborn position while still saving face.

Other children sometimes overcome their resistance if

toilet teaching is taken over by someone new. One family found that their late bloomer started using the potty when a friend of the family invited her to come along to the bathroom. And in another case, a mother who was at the end of her rope decided to wash her hands of the whole business and leave it to her husband. To everyone's surprise, the child's difficulties rapidly disappeared.

If these or other methods don't work for you, it's probably a good idea to get professional help if your late bloomer doesn't bloom by age four.

*Getting professional help*: If you need help for a problem that doesn't resolve itself with time, try to put aside feelings of distrust and defensiveness that may interfere with getting that help. It is an unfortunate fact that most families do not seek counseling when they need it for elimination difficulties with their children. Those who are able to accept assistance, however, generally experience a great sense of relief.

Many parents do not know how to find a therapist to help with problems like bed-wetting, soiling, or late toilet learning, and often there is no one around to give good advice. To address this problem, Dr. Charles E. Schaefer offers a free telephone consultation service for professionals and parents. An expert in the field, he will refer parents to a psychologist in their area who has special experience with children's toileting problems. Parents may call or write Dr. Schaefer at 540 Scarsdale Road, Yonkers, N.Y. 10707, telephone: 914-793-1532.

While it is unlikely that a resistance is a sign of deep-seated emotional problems, the child who is not helped to overcome a toilet-learning block that continues past the toddler years will surely suffer some loss of self-esteem. The obvious relief and pride of children who do learn after a long period of trouble tells how unhappy they must have

# Common Difficulties During Toilet Learning

felt before. The mother of one such little girl said, "She's very, very proud. She speaks with scorn: 'Only babies wear diapers.' And in a restaurant, she even leaned over and said to the man at the next table, 'Guess what? I go BM in the potty!'"

# 8. How Parents' Feelings and Attitudes Affect Toilet Teaching

Usually, the emphasis in toilet teaching is on the child, and this is how it should be. After all, he is the one who is learning. Sometimes, however, in concentrating on the child's behavior, the parents are completely overlooked and this is *not* as it should be, because parents are very much a part of the learning process.

Children, especially very young children, unconsciously pick up and reflect their parents' feelings. When a couple is having marital trouble, their child may be angry at the day-care center. When a mother is depressed, her toddler may seem quiet and listless. When parents are feeling happy and optimistic, their child is usually happy too.

Because of this constant, unspoken flow of feelings between parents and toddler, you are never uninvolved in your child's toilet learning, whether she is "making no progress" or "handling it all herself." To a large extent, we provide the emotional ambience within which our children live and learn. And learning to understand and accept our feelings—whatever they are—can help us and our children as well.

*Accepting our feelings and imperfections*: Sometimes people balk at exploring their emotions because they think they can't do anything about the way they feel. They're right. We can't help feeling the way we do and we shouldn't try.

But it is surprising how often just realizing what we are feeling can help. Coming face to face with an "unacceptable" feeling may be painful, but it is also a relief—we don't have to push the emotion away anymore. And accepting all sides of ourselves—the good, the bad, the small, and petty—makes us whole people, more real, and more alive.

In addition, getting in touch with a feeling in all its intensity can help to defuse it. Recognizing one's impatience, anger, shame, depression, laziness, or competitiveness is the first step in handling it. We don't necessarily have to change, but we don't have to act on our every impulse either. If we can experience the emotions, instead of denying them, we'll be less likely to put the burden of our own hang-ups on our children's shoulders.

*Some parental attitudes can interfere*: Some of our unconscious attitudes, character traits, and old feelings from childhood can interfere with our role as helpful guides to our toddlers. Feeling guilty about these ideas and emotions, disliking ourselves for them, or watching every move we make will only introduce more negatives into our lives and take away the spontaneity that is a positive force in child rearing. Simply being aware of some common attitudes and feelings, however, and understanding how they may affect a toddler during toilet teaching can make a difference:

—*Perfectionism*: People who are very careful to do everything "just right" can expect to run into some inner conflicts during toilet teaching. In the abstract, you may know that there will be a lot of trial and error, but if you're used to demanding perfection from yourself—and by extension from your child—the errors will be hard to accept. Similarly, if you like to be in control of everything, you may feel helpless when confronted with the inescapable fact that you can't control your child's elimination for him.

A mother who had these attitudes said, "I was so terrified that I would do it wrong. I actually felt that I would mess up Sam for life unless I did everything perfectly. So every time he had an accident, I felt as if it was the end of the world—because it showed that I wasn't the perfect mother, and because it was 'evidence' in my mind that things were going wrong. As a result, Sam got very, very tense. In the end, my husband took over, and then Sam was fine. He had an okay time learning to use the toilet. *I* had a terrible time."

Another parent, who liked everything to be perfectly neat and clean, preferred diapers because they prevented messy accidents and because she hated going into public toilets, which usually fell far below her standard of cleanliness. She found herself dreading toilet teaching because she knew she would have to put up with more mess than she could easily tolerate.

If you have feelings like these, take your temperament into account before beginning toilet teaching. Work on trying to realize that things can be good even if they aren't perfect—including your own parenting skills! Try to allow yourself some imperfections, and understand that it is *you* who are your own severest judge. No one else expects you to be perfect; others are willing to accept and like you as a "mere mortal."

On the practical side, you should be extra sure that your child is really ready before beginning toilet teaching, perhaps waiting until he is closer to three than two, when the learning period is likely to be shorter and easier. It is also very important for your spouse to take an active part, so that you will have support. The more pressure you can take off yourself, the calmer things will be and the easier toilet learning will be for you and your child.

—*Shame*: Mention something in conversation about bathrooms or toilets and your listeners are almost certain to make a joke. Much of this kind of humor stems from a sense of shame that was instilled in us as very young children by parents, teachers, and other children. One mother, discussing her feelings about toilet teaching, told an anecdote about herself as a child that many of us can probably identify with: "I remember the incident clearly. I was in kindergarten and I didn't get to the bathroom on time. The teacher asked, 'Who made this puddle?' and there was a trail of urine that led right to my chair. We all sat there on our hands, and I never admitted that I'd done it, even though it was so clear that I had. I would have died rather than confess to it openly."

Most of us can recall similar embarrassing moments in childhood, but nowadays, when people are so much more relaxed, we have outgrown such childish feelings—or have we? Coming of age in a more permissive environment has helped people overcome many of the inhibitions their parents had, but if we learned as children to be uncomfortable about our bodies or to think that anything relating to the genitals or elimination was shameful or disgusting, then these ideas may still influence our deepest feelings about ourselves.

# How Parents' Feelings / Attitudes Affect Toilet Teaching

Fortunately, there is a simple way to avoid handing down these negative attitudes to our children: just don't say anything negative about sex, the body, or elimination—ever. Whatever our own feelings or qualms may be, we should always refer to body parts by their correct names—penis, breast, vagina, etc.—in a matter-of-fact way. We should never shame a child for sex play or toileting accidents, and never express dislike toward the body or its products. We shouldn't say "ick" or "stinky," turn our heads away, wrinkle up our noses, or make any other expression of disgust when changing a diaper or cleaning up an accident.

—*Discipline*: Parents who pride themselves on having obedient children may find toilet teaching a frustrating experience. A toddler who is learning toileting is engaged in a process of gaining control that has little to do with discipline in the authoritarian sense of the word. He does need his parents' guidance in telling him what is expected, but apart from this gentle discipline, what he needs even more is to feel that he—and not the parents—is in control of his body. If a toddler senses that his own control is threatened by too much interference, his instinctive response will be to resist, which produces the opposite results from what the parents want. Indeed, stern methods that emphasize quick compliance can be found at the root of many elimination problems in older children.

If you are inclined to see toilet learning as a disciplinary matter, it may help if you try to think of it in a different way. When a baby is learning to walk, he is not punished for falling down, and the same principle should hold for toilet learning. Just as a toddler doesn't fall down to defy his parents, he doesn't have toileting accidents for that reason either. It's best to channel any disciplinary impulses in more appropriate directions and use only encouragement in toilet teaching.

—*Impatience*: If the label on the can of plant food says "add one teaspoon," are you tempted to add two teaspoons so the plant will grow faster? If so, your patience may be tried while teaching your child to use the toilet. You can't hurry growing things—plants or toddlers. You'll get better results by tuning in to the natural growth rate and rhythm of the organism than by trying to speed it up to match your desire for quick results.

Your patience may also be tried if you have negative feelings about changing diapers. Hardly anyone enjoys changing a messy diaper, but some people have more tolerance for it than others. If you feel like Cinderella chained to the changing table, it may not be easy to view toilet learning as a developmental step that will come when the child is ready. And if you are expecting a second baby, you may be feeling a bit frantic at the thought of changing two sets of diapers.

Feelings of impatience are natural and almost all parents have them. If we aren't careful, however, our impatience can have the opposite effect from the one we want. A toddler is in a naturally oppositional stage of life; if he senses an urgency in his parent's feelings, or if he feels hurt and rejected by her impatience, he may just dig in his heels and refuse to budge. Probably the best way for a parent to deal with such feelings is to accept them wholeheartedly. If you do tend to be impatient, sympathize with yourself and tell anyone who will listen how wildly impatient you are. At the same time, however, zealously guard against letting any of your impatience slip out to your child. It might also help if you and your spouse share the diaper detail as much as possible. And do keep in mind that infancy doesn't last forever, even though it may seem to have no end while it's in progress.

—*Competitiveness*: If your child is later than your neighbor's, you have probably told yourself that children mature at different rates and that some children are simply earlier than others. But for all your efforts at being rational, you may still feel like the mother who said, "I thought my son was a failure. If his friend could do it, why couldn't he?"

Another woman said she spent so much time obsessively comparing her child to others in the neighborhood that her exasperated husband finally said, "Toilet teaching is not a competitive sport!"

If a competition over toilet learning develops between you and other parents, it may help to realize that the game can't take place unless more than one party is willing to play. Your friends may be competing with you, but *you* are competing right back. Try to get in touch with the real reason for the competition. Do you think that unless you are better than other parents, you are not a good parent? Realize that your friends must have similar insecurities or they wouldn't be competing with you. And keep in mind that even if we could prove that we are better than everyone else, it doesn't mean that we would be better liked or accepted.

It can also help to realize that the children and their toileting have *nothing to do* with the adults' competition. It's the *parents* who want to be better than each other and they're just using the children in the contest. If you must compete, do it directly—compare incomes, cars, furniture, noses, whatever—but stop worrying about whose toddler is still in diapers.

—*Overcompensation*: Sometimes a parent may try to compensate for what she sees as a flaw in herself by correcting her child. In talking about the pressure she put on her son for perfect behavior in toilet learning, a mother admitted, "I tend to be a little slovenly and lazy myself, and I don't want my child to be like that. So I'm often a little harder on him than I should be."

Another mother went the other way trying to compensate for the "flaw" in her character: "I know I am obsessive, self-critical and very achievement oriented, and so I was afraid of toilet teaching. I knew if I followed my natural inclinations, I would be rigid and pressuring. Also, part of me hates that side of myself and I don't want my daughter to be like that. So I bent over backward to be relaxed about toilet teaching. I was completely *laissez-faire* and afraid to make any demands on my little 'noble savage.'"

Such overcompensation really isn't appropriate because the corrective measures are being applied to the wrong person: to the child instead of the parent. The *parent* is the one who needs more discipline, more nurturing, more whatever. We should be suspicious of anything we do just so our children won't be like us, and we should try to direct impulses for improvement toward ourselves. What a child needs most from his parents is to be seen as he is and treated accordingly.

—*Doubts about independence and development*: Sometimes inner conflicts about toilet teaching arise over issues of independence and growth. We rely on our own parents as role models in parenting, and if we weren't encouraged to develop independence naturally as children, we won't have an instinct about how to foster it in our own children. In other words, we won't trust our children to grow and learn without a lot of prodding and pushing.

Those adults whose mothers and fathers pressured them to be independent too early, or, conversely, expected them to remain dependent for too long, may have a more difficult time achieving a balance between giving children help when they need it and supporting independence when they are ready for it.

One young woman said, "My mother talks about how I could put on my own snowsuit when I was two years old, when my brother was born. I remember feeling that I was always being pushed to be big ánd grown up. I know I have done similar things to my child," she added ruefully, "especially by being too harsh in toilet teaching."

Another woman, who was encouraged to remain over-dependent, said, "My mother tended to reinforce my weaknesses. If I was shy about going to a party, she'd say I didn't have to go. If I was nervous about trying something new, that was reason enough to give up. At the time, I thought I was abnormally timid, but now I think I just wasn't encouraged enough.

"I have tried not to be like that with my own daughter, but I know I sometimes treat her the way my mother treated me. For instance, I sometimes feel doubtful about her abilities, although realistically I know she is bright. As incredible as it sounds, I think I wondered deep down if she would be *able* to learn to use the toilet. Maybe that was why I hesitated for a while before beginning toilet teaching."

Since toilet learning is in many ways a child's first step toward autonomy and self-control, it is perhaps the first time parents are confronted so squarely with their own attitudes toward these issues. Those who haven't had the opportunity to learn by example to encourage a child's steps toward autonomy may find it difficult to foster a gradual movement from the dependence of infancy to the relative independence of childhood. Instead, they may tend to push their child too hard or to hold him back by subtly communicating low expectations. However, they'll find it easier to achieve a balance once they have experienced enough positive growth in their own lives. It's also helpful to learn what types of independent behavior can be expected of children at various ages. Some books that provide such information on child development are *Infant and Child in the Culture of Today* by Arnold Gesell, M.D., Frances L.

Ilg, M.D., and Louise Bates Ames, Ph.D., and a series of paperbacks by Ames and Ilg entitled *Your One-Year-Old*, *Your Two-Year-Old*, and so on up to age six. The detailed descriptions of typical behavior, abilities, and limitations can help parents determine whether they are demanding too much or too little of their child for his age.

*Between husband and wife*: In most households in the past, toilet teaching was considered the wife's job, as were most duties involving babies and young children. Today things are different. Many fathers are taking an active role in parenting right from the start, and their participation is resulting in closer relationships and more cooperation in family life.

Some husbands and wives very consciously help each other with their individual parenting bugbears. A wife may tactfully bail her husband out when he is trying to use reason instead of distraction to keep a one-year-old from pestering the cat. And a husband may rescue his wife when the bedtime giggles have all but exhausted her patience. Similarly, spouses who share the job of parenting will serve as each other's sounding board, reassure each other when worries grow out of proportion, and pool their knowledge and skills to solve everyday problems.

Occasionally, however, a difficulty may arise in a family when a couple cannot agree on a common toilet-teaching policy. One spouse may want to start early, while the other prefers to wait, or one may practice punishing or shaming, which the other cannot tolerate.

Certainly, couples need not present a united front on every question regarding their child, but basic differences between parents over an important issue like toilet teaching can confuse a child. She may be torn between conflicting loyalites to each parent or she may not be sure what is really expected of her, and these uncertainties can interfere with her learning. Before going ahead with toilet teaching, it's important for parents to try to resolve any differences of opinion in private.

One way of dealing with differences is for both parents to agree to read the same one or two child-care books and then discuss them. It isn't necessary that the parents agree with the books, nor is it essential that they agree whole-heartedly with each other—they may have to compromise. But if the discussion is based on common knowledge of child-rearing practices and the reasons behind them, chances are that it will be more or less constructive, and the parents will be able to agree on one fairly consistent policy to follow.

*Getting support and avoiding pressure from others*: While a husband and wife need to agree with one another on some level in order to raise children together, interference from relatives and friends is another matter. Many parents of toddlers experience pressure and even outright hostility from their own parents and parents-in-law.

"My wife's mother talks about how she trained her children at five months" said one young father, "and that's supposed to mean 'Why can't *you* do that?'"

Another father told about his parents' disapproval of waiting until the child was two and a half to begin toilet teaching: "They think it's a scandal. They think we're terribly neglectful parents. They feel that if Debra didn't work (another scandal!) then she could sit in the bathroom with Joey every two hours and make him go."

Obviously, these young families cannot yield to the advice of their parents, whose ideas about toilet teaching differ so much from their own. But even if you have no intention of changing your behavior, pressure and disapproval can be hard to take. You may just have to grin and bear it, but sometimes telling others honestly how you feel—without attacking them—can enlist their cooperation in place of criticism.

"I told my parents that I felt watched and judged," said a mother. "They seemed to react well when I said that parenting was a hard job and I wished we could have their support and help instead of their disapproval."

And there seem to be as many grandparents who are aware of new ideas in child rearing and sensitive to the need of young parents to make their own decisions. One woman related, "My mother asked, 'Aren't you starting toilet training yet?' and I said, 'No' and told her why. She accepted it and never mentioned it again." Another parent said, "It turns out that my mother-in-law is my friend. I'm extraordinarily lucky about this. I ask her for advice. She raised three children, and this is my first child, so I'd be crazy not to."

Probably the most frequent source of help and support comes from talking with other parents who have children of the same age. It means a lot to share the pleasures and troubles of parenting with others who are going through the same experiences, if you can get past the defensiveness that often interferes with mutual support.

A mother whose son had gone through a period of having BMs in his pants recalled that her defensiveness had led her to misunderstand a friend's effort to be helpful: "Here I was with two kids—an infant who was keeping me up around the clock and a toddler who wouldn't use the toilet. And I was very hurt when my friend said, 'Gee, it's nice not to have to change diapers anymore.' Later I learned that she didn't mean it the way I took it. She was trying to say, 'It'll happen to you. Don't worry about him.' But at the time, I was so hypersensitive that I assumed she was putting me down, turned away, and couldn't accept her help."

A father spoke of how his experience in a parents' discussion group helped him overcome his defensiveness: "I was terrified to talk about my anger at my son, which seemed so monstrous to me (how could I be so mad at a defenseless little kid?) when the father sitting next to me suddenly described *identical* feelings that he had toward his child. I was so relieved, and after that, I was never defensive about bringing anything up. I discovered that the less defensive you can be about things like this, the more help you are going to get from other people, because they'll feel freer to discuss the same sensitive subjects with you."

Parents who needed guidance with toilet teaching reported that they got help from such sources as pediatricians, psychologists, and day-care center and nursery school personnel. But often what we need most is not so much professional advice as a good listener, someone to give us the support we need in handling our own feelings and maintaining the calm, matter-of-fact attitude that best fosters a child's successful toilet learning.

# 9. Putting Things in Perspective

While it is going on, parents may think about it quite a lot. But once it has been accomplished, it fades rapidly into the past, and they hardly ever think about it again. That is one of the nice things about toilet teaching.

Still, the experience of teaching your child to use the toilet does not disappear entirely. When asked if they had gained anything from toilet teaching, most parents simply laughed at first. But when pressed to consider the question, many realized that they had undergone some important changes in attitudes and parenting skills. Perhaps the most common gain parents reported was a sense of perspective about time.

"You think it's going to go on forever," said one mother, "then all of a sudden it's over. It's hard for me to remember now why I thought it was such a big deal whether he was

**111**

out of diapers at twenty-eight months or thirty-one months. Three more months of diapers in a lifetime—what difference does it make? But then, I felt it was a life-or-death situation."

Another parent said, "I realize now that things will happen if you just give them a chance. But you have to *let* them happen—you can't force things just to suit your convenience."

Looking back, parents in general felt that they had been too tense, had not had enough faith that their children would learn in a reasonable time, and had put too much pressure on their children. They could easily see how these gains in insight and experience would help them with toilet teaching in the future. Many parents shared the conviction of the father who said, "We won't worry so much and we won't start so early with the second child."

Another parent pointed out that she would apply what she had learned in toilet teaching to other learning situations as her child grows older. "I can see now that I don't have to feel panicked because he doesn't know how to tie his shoes yet or because he can't hold a pencil properly. Before, I may have worried or thought, 'If I don't make sure he learns this right now, he'll *never* do it right.' But now I know he will learn in his own time, when he's ready."

A mother who had become "overinvested," as she put it, in her son's learning and had lost her temper many times, realized that her emotional response had not been helpful. "All my yelling and all my craziness didn't help either one of us. Now I realize that he 'toughed it out.' He learned in spite of me!"

Some people even found that they had gained personally, not just as parents but as individuals.

"This is really on a basic level," confided one woman, "but being a parent, being so involved in my child's learning to use the toilet, and having her communicate to me so easily and openly about it helped me get over being uptight myself. I'm not as embarrassed about using the bathroom as I used to be, and I feel a lot freer about everything physical. This even extends to my sexual life, too."

Another parent attributed a change in her attitude toward her own growth to the experience of toilet teaching and parenting in general. "Watching my daughter develop and learn has given me more faith in my own ability to grow and learn. I had to be patient with her, and now I am more patient with myself. I'll give myself a second chance and a third chance, instead of getting impatient and giving up. As a result, I've done more things that I wanted to do and accomplished more than I did before. From parenting my child, I've learned how to treat myself."

Even parents who recalled tense times during regressions and resistances, and even a mother who at first said, "Toilet teaching? I did a terrible job of it!" realized after the experience was over that they had gained new insight into parenting and themselves.

And parents whose experiences had been smoother tended to agree with the mother who said, "I was glad to have the confirmation of what I already believed: that children want to learn and want to grow up, and they will do it if you support them and give them a chance."

# 10. Questions Parents Frequently Ask: A Review

*When do most children learn to use the toilet?*

According to a recent study, the *average* age for learning to use the potty or toilet reliably for bowel and bladder is twenty-eight months. Although it is important to remember that each child is an individual and develops at his own rate, generally speaking, you can expect your child to achieve daytime control sometime between the ages of two and three, and nighttime control between three and four-and-a-half.

*Should I begin toilet teaching early to give my child a headstart?*

No. Toilet teaching is best started around the time the child becomes ready to learn and able to control his elimination. Most children do not have the physical ability to control their bowels before about eighteen months, and they do not achieve bladder control until sometime later. Beginning toilet teaching early simply causes frustration for the parent and puts unnecessary pressure on a young toddler. Too early toilet teaching can actually delay progress rather than encourage it.

*Should I leave toilet learning up to my child and avoid making any demands of her?*

No. Toddlers need to know what their parents expect of them. You should not push or pressure your child, but do watch for signs of readiness, prepare her gradually by teaching her about toileting over a period of time, and communicate very clearly that you have confidence that she will learn to use the potty and toilet when she is ready.

*What are the signs of readiness for toilet learning?*

A toddler may show some—but not necessarily all—of the following signs as he becomes ready for learning: pausing and making sounds and grimaces while having a BM; being regular in bowel movements; staying dry for an hour or two in the daytime; waking up dry from a nap; complaining when wet or soiled; being aware that urine and feces come from his body; telling the parent when he has had or is having a BM; generally liking to be clean and tidy; and wanting to imitate adults and be grown up.

*How can I prepare my child for toilet learning?*

In the course of your everyday activities, point out when she is having a BM or is urinating; teach her that urine and feces come from her body; teach her the words you want her to use for bathroom functions; allow her to observe others using the toilet and explain what it is for; read her a children's book about toilet learning; mention the advantages of staying clean and dry; get a potty and introduce it as her own possession; let her practice using the potty and praise her for success; mention that when she is bigger, she will start using the potty all the time and will wear underpants "like a big girl."

*When should I expect my child to stop wearing diapers and use the potty or toilet in the daytime?*

When your toddler is between the ages of two and three, has shown some signs of readiness, and has had an ample period of preparation, you can expect him to become interested in giving up diapers. Switch from diapers to pants for waking activities if he: (1) occasionally asks to have his diaper removed so he can use the potty; (2) tells you he wants underpants and doesn't want to wear diapers anymore; or (3) has shown clearly that he is physically able to control elimination.

*What should I do about accidents?*

Expect a child to have accidents for a while after she starts to use the potty and be relaxed about them. Accidents are a normal part of toilet learning and a child should not be shamed or punished when she has one. Clean up calmly, and reassure her that next time she'll remember to use the potty. During the day, give gentle reminders to use the potty to help her have as much success as possible.

*If my child has been clean and dry for a while and suddenly begins having many accidents, what should I do?*

Regressions to wetting and/or soiling are not uncommon in toddlers and are usually a reaction to stress. Look for sources of pressure in the child's life—separation from a parent, a new baby, starting nursery school, moving, etc.— and try to ease tension by providing reassurance. Staying patient, understanding, and calm are the best ways for dealing with regressions, which usually go away by themselves in a short time. A child should not be punished for a loss of control.

*When should I expect my child to stay dry at night?*

Staying dry while sleeping usually comes several months after daytime control is established, but many normal children, especially boys, take longer to achieve dry nights. The best way to handle night wetting is to be patient and wait for the child's bladder to mature. Punitive methods are definitely harmful. Praise your child for any dry nights he may have; make no comment about wet beds; and express your confidence that he will be having more dry nights as he grows older.

*When should I start to worry about a "late bloomer"?*

If your child has not achieved daytime control by three and a half to four, and/or is not making progress in controlling night wetting after age five, it is wise to consult your physician to rule out any physical causes, and then a child psychologist to help your child overcome the difficulties.

# Questions Parents Frequently Ask: A Review

*What parental attitudes and behavior will most encourage successful toilet learning?*

Psychologists say that parents whose children learn to use the toilet most easily are calm and patient and show a matter-of-fact attitude toward toilet teaching; communicate clearly what behavior is expected of the child; anticipate gradual, rather than instant, success; do not use negative tactics like punishment, scolding, or shaming; observe the child and try to wait until he expresses interest in toilet learning; encourage and praise the child for successes and are understanding about accidents; switch from diapers to pants when the child is ready; are not hesitant but send a clear message that they have confidence in the child's ability to learn.

# Index

121

# Index

123

# Index

# Index

# About the Author

A graduate of the City College of New York with a B.A. in psychology, Joanna Cole is a former elementary school teacher, letters correspondent for *Newsweek*, and senior editor for Doubleday Books for Young Readers. She is now a full-time writer, specializing in books and articles for and about children.

She is married to Philip Cole, a psychotherapist. They have a daughter, Rachel, and live in New York City.